# FROM THE VAULT
## Stories You Probably Never Knew About South Carolina Methodism

# FROM THE VAULT
## Stories You Probably Never Knew About South Carolina Methodism

Dr. Phillip Stone

South Carolina United Methodist Advocate Press, Columbia, South Carolina
Copyright © 2024 by South Carolina United Methodist Advocate Press

All rights reserved. No part of this book may be reproduced or transmitted in any form or by any means, electronic or mechanical, including photocopying, recording or by any information storage and retrieval system, without permission in writing from the Publisher.

First published in the United States of America in 2024 by the South Carolina United Methodist Advocate Press.

Library of Congress Cataloging-in-Publication Data
From the Vault
p. cm.

ISBN 978-1-966237-04-4

*To Rev. Luther H. Rickenbaker III, for his many years of service as the senior research associate in the conference archives, and to local church historians, for doing the ministry of memory in their local churches.*

# Table of Contents

Foreword by Dr. A. V. Huff Jr., conference historian .............................. ix
Introduction: Our Connection and Our Stories ................................ xi

## Section 1: Advice for the Church Historian
Chapter 1: What Is an Archives? ............................................................. 3
Chapter 2: The Local Church Historian ................................................ 5
Chapter 3: What Should We Put in Our History Room? ...................... 7
Chapter 4: Living Through History ....................................................... 9

## Section 2: People
Chapter 5: Bishop Joseph B. Bethea .................................................... 13
Chapter 6: Bishop William Capers ....................................................... 15
Chapter 7: Bishop Roy C. Clark ........................................................... 19
Chapter 8: Bishop Collins Denny ......................................................... 21
Chapter 9: Bishop William Wallace Duncan ...................................... 23
Chapter 10: Bishop Paul Hardin Jr. ...................................................... 25
Chapter 11: Bishop John C. Kilgo ........................................................ 27
Chapter 12: Bishop Edwin D. Mouzon ............................................... 29
Chapter 13: Bishop A. Coke Smith ...................................................... 31
Chapter 14: Bishop John Owen Smith ................................................ 33
Chapter 15: Bishop James S. Thomas .................................................. 35
Chapter 16: Bishop Edward L. Tullis ................................................... 37
Chapter 17: Bishop William M. Wightman ........................................ 39
Chapter 18: Reverend James Belin ....................................................... 41
Chapter 19: President James H. Carlisle .............................................. 43
Chapter 20: President Henry Nelson Snyder ...................................... 45
Chapter 21: Maria Davies Wightman
      and the Woman's Missionary Society ............................. 47
Chapter 22: Mary Belle Winn: Missionary to China ......................... 49
Chapter 23: Louise Best: Missionary to Brazil .................................... 51
Chapter 24: Dr. Wil Lou Gray: Evangelist for Education ................... 55

## Section 3: Institutions
Chapter 25: The Birth of the *Advocate*, 1837 ..................................... 59
Chapter 26: Spartanburg Female College ............................................ 61
Chapter 27: South Carolina's Methodist Women's Colleges ............... 63

Chapter 28: The Conference Historical Society ........................................ 65
Chapter 29: Methodism and Textiles ........................................................ 67
Chapter 30: Women's Organizations ........................................................ 71

## Section 4: History
Chapter 31: The Sancho Letter ................................................................ 75
Chapter 32: Slavery and the First Great Methodist Schism, 1844 ......... 79
Chapter 33: The Beginning of the 1866 Conference .............................. 83
Chapter 34: Methodism and Race in South Carolina ............................ 85
Chapter 35: Dividing the Conference, 1914 ........................................... 87
Chapter 36: Methodist Reunification, 1939 ........................................... 89
Chapter 37: The First Southeastern Jurisdictional Conference ............. 93
Chapter 38: The 1964 General Conference ............................................ 95
Chapter 39: Selma 1965, as One Editor Saw It ...................................... 97
Chapter 40: The United Methodist Church Turns Fifty ....................... 99
Chapter 41: Prelude to Merger .............................................................. 101
Chapter 42: Becoming One Annual Conference ................................. 103
Chapter 43: South Carolina Methodism Enters the Seventies ............ 107
Chapter 44: Susanna Wesley: Mother of Methodism .......................... 109
Chapter 45: Charles Wesley: O For a Thousand Hymns? .................... 111
Chapter 46: The Women in John Wesley's Life ................................... 113

## Section 5: Communities
Chapter 47: Methodism in Charleston ................................................. 117
Chapter 48: Cokesbury, the Methodist Town ...................................... 123
Chapter 49: Methodism in Columbia ................................................... 125
Chapter 50: Early Methodism in Georgetown ..................................... 127
Chapter 51: The Beginning of Methodism in Greenville .................... 129
Chapter 52: Early Methodism in Spartanburg ..................................... 133
Chapter 53: Early Methodism in York County .................................... 135

## Section 6: Resources
Chapter 54: Histories of the Conference .............................................. 139
Chapter 55: Clergy Pictorial Directories .............................................. 141
Chapter 56: Conference Journals .......................................................... 143
Chapter 57: Historic Places in South Carolina .................................... 145

About the Author ................................................................................... 147

# Foreword

Dr. Phillip Stone occupies a unique place from which to view the long history of those whom John Wesley named "the people called Methodists" in the British province and later the state of South Carolina. He is the archivist of the South Carolina Conference of The United Methodist Church and presides over the Conference Archives at Wofford College in Spartanburg. He also works with the staff of the Conference Archives housed at Claflin University in Orangeburg.

In addition to his archival work, Phillip is an adjunct member of the Wofford College faculty and teaches courses in the history and politics of South Carolina. As a lifelong member of Spartanburg's Bethel United Methodist Church, he is responsible for the archives of a local church, as well.

Originating as columns written for the *South Carolina United Methodist Advocate*, the essays here cover a wide variety of useful and topics. They range from the work of maintaining a local church archive to treatment of crucial events in the life of the annual conference. He also introduces us to a number of Methodist leaders who have served as bishops, pastors, missionaries, and lay leaders.

If you read first where your interest leads you, you will gain a wide appreciation for the twists and turns of Methodism in South Carolina.

*Dr. A. V. Huff Jr.*
*Conference Historian*

# Introduction
## Our Connection and Our Stories

The story of American Methodism includes both unity and disunity. Today's United Methodist Church is the product of several mergers, including large ones in 1939 and 1968. It has had divisions in its past, including the separation over slavery in 1844. At other times, segments that have disagreed with the church's treatment of various groups have departed. Some other Methodist denominations, such as the African Methodist Episcopal Church, represent parts of our tradition that left because of what they perceived as unequal treatment by members of the Methodist Episcopal Church in the early nineteenth century.

I offer this as a preface that separation and unification are nothing new in our church's history. Part of what our archives can do is tell the stories of how these changes happened.

Another role of the archives is to show us all the ways we are connected. Our connection is a central part of our history and our theology as Methodists, so celebrating that connection has been a consistent theme of my work as the conference's archivist. The archives connects us to our past, but it also connects us to our future, for without someone to preserve the records of the past and present, the future won't have any history.

The mandate of our conference archives is to collect the permanently valuable records of the South Carolina Conference of The United Methodist Church annual conference and its agencies, and at the same time, to collect materials about the history of Methodism and Methodists in South Carolina. So in addition to the conference journals, *South Carolina United Methodist Advocate* editions, records of boards and commissions, and closed church records, we also look for books about Methodism, histories of local churches, and the papers of various clergy or laity who are connected with Methodism in the state.

Some of what connects us are the documents themselves. We have issues of the *Advocate* back to 1837, and from them we can learn how Methodists struggled over contentious issues. The minutes of the conference, available in print and digitally, tell of the actions of the annual conference over the years. Many of the original handwritten minutes from the nineteenth century must have traveled around the state with the various secretaries. These minutes show the names of individuals who built the church and who responded to God's call. They show the care that secretaries took to make sure the records of their work were preserved.

For me, the records are about our stories. It's important not to lose sight of the stories that abound in our collections—and these are the things that can be the most rewarding to share. Documents such as these can give our researchers a powerful sense of history. They help us see our connection to the past.

One of my favorite items in the collection is a letter to a former bishop that's an allegorical complaint about the minister being moved—written on toilet tissue. I am sure some clergy could relate to the minister's reaction. Other favorites are the *Devil's Advocate*, a satirical underground publication of the 1960s and 1970s. At some point, I'm going to need some help in interpreting all the inside jokes in those papers. The letters of missionary Mary Belle Winn, a South Carolinian who worked in China from 1923 to 1949, which describe her life and work in the mission field, represent a fascinating look at the church's overseas work. And a letter describing the life and experiences of a slave named Sancho, who was converted to Methodism by Bishop Francis Asbury, also tells a powerful story of forgiveness. These stories get to the very heart of our experiences as Methodists in South Carolina.

Beginning in the summer of 2012, I realized I needed a way to tell more of our stories, but also to help Methodists in our conference understand more about the work of the Commission on Archives and History. I also felt an obligation to help local church historians and others who are interested in history to do their jobs better. I asked *Advocate* Editor Jessica Brodie if I could write a column each month, and she immediately agreed. I had just started serving on the *Advocate* Board of Trustees, so it seemed like a natural extension of my work. For the past twelve years, I've produced about 128 monthly columns, though from time to time, I've missed a month.

A year or so ago, while serving on the Advocate Press committee, I read a manuscript that inspired me to collect some of these columns, lightly edit them, and publish them as a collection. I've sorted these columns into a few categories. The book begins with some articles that give advice to local church historians on how to arrange a history room and how to think about their work. The next sections largely contain biographical selections and articles about conference institutions or Methodist history. A few columns talk about Methodist history in some communities in the state. The last section talks about resources that are available in the archives and online.

This collection is not comprehensive. I've left out some things, and I haven't written a historical column about every community in the state. I realized as I was compiling the columns that I'd never written about several of our institutions.

The great part of that is it gives me ideas for things to write about in the next twelve years.

*Dr. Phillip Stone*
*October 2024*

# Section 1

## Advice for the Church Historian

These columns talk about what archives are, the role of the local church historian, and what sorts of things can be included in a history room if your church has such a space. It also includes some suggestions for how to respond to current historical events.

# Chapter 1
## What Is an Archives?

Archives conjure up all sorts of images, and in many peoples' minds, they usually involve dust.

Maybe you're thinking of a warehouse of boxes, or a small, dark room near the top floor of a building, with someone, probably of advanced age, there to help find some hard-to locate bit of information. Or maybe you're thinking of that large Gothic room with the tall windows, long tables, green table lamps, and rows of bookshelves filled with heavy volumes.

The truth is, we don't really like dust, and we try to keep the books and papers in the various collections as free of it as possible. Archives vary in size, from closet to warehouse. And the types of things in archives aren't limited to books but can range from paper files to audio recordings and video tape, from maps to computer files, and from yearbooks to photographs.

Technically, archives are the permanently valuable records of an organization, such as a college, a church, a state, or an annual conference. In our case, they include the conference journals, the *Advocate*, some conference board and commission minutes such as the Commission on the Status and Role of Women, the Commission on Worship, the Board of Higher Education and Campus Ministry, along with some agency files and district records. We have the conference United Women in Faith's archives.

An archives might also collect materials that relate to its mission, such as books by and about South Carolina Methodism or Methodists, pictorial directories, local church histories, and files on different churches. Taking a broader view, archives to some people are simply the place where the old stuff goes, or where one goes for information about the past.

Our primary focus is on the records of the annual conference, though we do have the records of some closed local churches. If you are looking for local church history, the best place to start is in the local church, the community, or the public library, though we may be able to help with some statistics, a list of pastoral appointments, and changes in charge lines. We've put pictures of clergy online so local churches can download them. Some researchers call to ask if we can produce an ancestor's baptism or marriage record. I wish it were that easy. We don't have the baptism or marriage records for active congregations, nor do we have their church council minutes. If we tried to keep all of that, we would need a warehouse, and anyone who has visited knows we don't have that kind of space!

Why should your church have an archives? In part, because keeping local church history is the local church's responsibility. That's why you might have a local church historian and a committee on records and history. The church historian's job is to take care of the church's historical records and to make sure that records being produced today—everything from the weekly bulletin or newsletter to the minutes of the church council—are being kept in a safe place.

You can find help from the conference archives website or from the General Commission on Archives and History's website. GCAH gives plenty of guidance on how to organize a local church archives.

And you can always contact me for guidance. I'll even remind you to keep the dust out.

# Chapter 2
## The Local Church Historian

January means a new year for many church officers, and that means that some churches may have a new person in the office of local church historian. If so, I hope some of these suggestions will help you figure out what you've agreed to do!

You might be thinking that you suddenly must write a history of your church. That's probably not the place to start, unless you, unlike most of us, have boundless amounts of time. In truth, your job is a blend of being an archivist and a historian. You are responsible for preserving the church's historical records as well as interpreting them for the congregation.

Section 247.5 of the *United Methodist Book of Discipline* talks about the duties of the church historian. The Discipline strongly recommends that each charge conference "elect a church historian in order to preserve the history of each local church." The Discipline says the church historian may be a member of the church council and may also hold another office at the same time.

The church historian is responsible for keeping the historical records of the church up-to-date and for the preservation of all local church records and historical materials no longer in current use. Those are the biggest responsibilities. The historian chairs the Committee on Records and History, if there is one, and provides an annual report on the care of church records and historical materials to the charge conference.

What does it mean to keep the church's records? The *Book of Discipline* makes the local church responsible for its records. The most important records that churches should be keeping include membership records, including baptisms and marriages, and the business records of the church, such as the minutes of charge conference, church council, committees, budgets, and audits. Other items, such as the newsletter or worship bulletin, programs from events, photographs, church directories, and even newspaper clippings can be worth keeping. Any insurance policies, contracts, or active files should be kept in the church office and not in the archives. Bills, vouchers, and giving records are not archival materials and can be safely destroyed after a few years. Many churches may have older records, such as old membership registers or quarterly conference ledgers. These are archival materials and should be maintained, preferably in a safe space.

Church records need to be kept in a secure space that is climate-controlled. Try to keep heat, moisture, and bright light away from the materials. A fireproof vault isn't necessary, but it is good if you have one. The main point here is to keep things in a place where they can't inadvertently disappear. Avoiding a place where a flood could happen is also a good idea.

Preserving and collecting records will help you in your other important duty, and that is to promote and interpret church history to the church. Every congregation, no matter its age, has a story, but you must have the documents that tell those stories. You should use your records to make members aware of past work that the church has done. It is a tribute to the saints who have upheld the church, and it may inspire members today to undertake some new mission. You may also want to ask members of the church to record their own memories of the church. For many of us, our church may be the one thing we're part of for our entire life. Those memories can be written or recorded and could be an interesting project for a group to undertake.

Many ways exist to promote and interpret the church's history. One is to put items in display cases where members can see some of what is in the history room. Another is to make presentations to groups in the church. Confirmation classes certainly should learn something about the church's history, as should new members. Celebrating Heritage Sunday, writing historical sketches for directories and bulletins, and being present in the life of the church are all ways that the church historian can promote and interpret Methodist history.

The main responsibility of the church historian is to use your gifts to help the members of your congregation learn more about your church and how it has evolved over the years. Of course, if you want to write a history of your church, then by all means, get to it!

# Chapter 3
## What Should We Put in Our History Room?

Maybe you've had a history room in your church for years. Maybe you've just recently managed to persuade the trustees to give you a small space to devote to history. Perhaps you are new to the job of church historian and are just trying to get your bearings. Whichever your situation is, you may be asking yourself what you should be doing with your history room.

The ideal room, as I've mentioned in the last chapter, is one where you can limit sunlight, heat, and humidity and can secure valuable artifacts and records. It's a room that has a stable climate, avoiding wild changes in temperature and humidity.

But what items might you collect for the room? Books, papers, newsletters, and photographs that tell the story of your congregation are always good candidates for your collection. Certainly, old church directories are a great resource. They're also very popular to show to confirmation classes, as I've experienced firsthand. The Sunday bulletins, weekly or monthly newsletters, and other letters or messages that go to the whole church are important for documenting the life of the church. Some of your records, such as membership rolls, may need to stay in the church office or in a safe. But others can easily find a home in the history room.

Other groups, such as the United Women in Faith or United Methodist Men, might be invited to place some of their records in the history room. You might also be on the lookout for materials from different Sunday school classes or other groups within the church. If a Sunday school class decides to disband, you can invite that class to place some of their memorabilia, such as class pictures, roll books, photographs, or artifacts, in the church history room. Doing so will give the congregation a way to recognize the ministry of that former group or Sunday school class. Don't forget to include photographs or artifacts from events important to the church, of events for which your church is known in your community.

Pictures, of course, are always popular. Pictures or posters about youth retreats, vacation Bible school, and church picnics can help your congregation remember those events. Try to save photos of special events, but don't forget about the photographs of recurring events, too. They are always good for displays but also to help show people what the church, the sanctuary, the parlor, or some other room looked like at various stages in the church's history.

Some congregations like to have a photo gallery of former ministers somewhere in the church. The history room might be a place for them if there is not any other option. If you are looking for photos of former ministers, the Conference Archives might be able to help. We've put many of them online.

The history room is a good way to use your imagination, so find a committee member who is creative and willing to help put together interesting displays.

What if we don't have a history room? Well, these suggestions can be your starting point when you do get one!

# Chapter 4
## Living Through History

*Author's note: I wrote this in spring 2020, when our churches had suspended in-person worship and many of us were working or learning from home:*

In addition to the history of the past, there is history we are all living through right now, as well as ways we can preserve today's history for the future.

History happens on ordinary days, and most of the time, it happens unexpectedly. Major events can change the world between breakfast and dinner, and historians spend years trying to understand and explain them. And in some cases, history unfolds over days and weeks and can have just as profound an effect on us.

I think that's what we're going through now. Part of the challenge with living through history is that we don't know the end of the story because it hasn't happened yet. I've pointed this out to students in my Western Civilization classes at Wofford when I talk about the outbreak of World War II in 1939. We have the advantage of hindsight, I like to point out. The British didn't know in the dark days of 1940 how the war was going to turn out, while we know how the story ends. That affects how we see those events, whereas they had to live with the uncertainty and fear of not knowing what was going to happen. So today, we are living with uncertainty.

Often, people probably think about archivists and historians as people who deal with the past. And part of what I do is to maintain the records of the past so that people today can appreciate where we've been, and I help people—genealogists, local church historians, conference staff—learn more about the past. However, archivists have to look forward as well, for if we don't collect the records of today, then archivists, historians, and other researchers in the future won't have any way to understand what we are going through right now.

So, as an archivist and historian, I have to be aware that we are making history right now, and make sure that it gets documented. That might mean keeping track of messages that get sent to the public. It might mean collecting news articles and other types of documents. It might involve asking others to be sure they are keeping good records of what's going on. It might even mean taking a more intentional act, like keeping a journal.

In addition to the routine things I have been doing, I decided a few weeks ago, actually at my mom's suggestion, to start keeping a journal. I try to take a few minutes each evening to write a few memories of the day. I don't know what I'll do with it in the end, but it might become part of my own file in the Wofford archives so that down the line, some future researcher will be able to see a little of what went on in Spartanburg and at Bethel Church and at Wofford during spring 2020. That's how historians a century from now will piece together what this experience was like—by reading the words of people who kept records.

So what can you do? You can keep a journal as well. Write about what happened today, what your own experience was, or how unusual everything seemed. Even mundane thoughts, added to those of others, might be able to paint a picture of life for someone in the future. You can make sure that your church is keeping an account of how it is dealing with this situation. What messages are going to members, how is your leadership managing the church's work? How is this affecting your members?

Beyond writing, take time to think and recognize what an unusual time this is. I certainly have never worked from home for weeks on end before, and I've never tried to figure out how to teach a class without seeing my students face to face. You are certainly doing things differently now, so reflect on that. I know that clergy are trying to figure out how to do ministry without seeing their congregations. What's that like for you?

Another thing to consider is how will this change us as individuals, communities, and a nation? What's going to be different in the future because of this experience?

Take some time to think, reflect, and maybe write some history of your own.

# Section 2

## People

These columns are about different people who have been influential in South Carolina Methodism. Some of them are bishops who served our conference, some are college presidents who were lay leaders in South Carolina and in the general church, and some are missionaries who have led in ministries.

# Chapter 5
## Bishop Joseph B. Bethea

In summer 1988, Bishop Joseph B. Bethea became the South Carolina Conference's new bishop.

Bishop Bethea's appointment to lead the South Carolina Conference was historic, as he became the first African American to lead the conference since the merger of the state's Black and White Methodist conferences in 1972.

A native of Dillon, South Carolina, Bethea was the son of a minister in the 1866 Conference, the Reverend Rufus Bethea, who died while serving Trinity Church in Camden. Bethea graduated from Claflin University and Gammon Theological Seminary, was ordained in 1956, and served some of his early appointments in South Carolina, at Walhalla and Ninety Six. He then moved to North Carolina and later Virginia, where he served local churches and was a superintendent of three different districts. He also served as director of Black Church Studies and a lecturer in preaching at Duke Divinity School, and as the administrative assistant to the bishop of the North Carolina Conference. He had been a candidate for bishop in previous years, but when he was elected on the twelfth ballot in 1988, he was only the second Black bishop elected by the Southeastern Jurisdiction.

The *Advocate* article announcing his election and appointment to South Carolina noted that the new bishop would make preaching a priority.

Bethea told the jurisdictional delegates he had four loves: God, his family, the church, and people. In his first *Advocate* column in September 1988, the new bishop emphasized a theme of coming home and giving thanks. He thanked all those who had helped him become a bishop and those who had welcomed him back to South Carolina. His formal installation was on Sept. 25 at Shandon Church.

Bethea's term in South Carolina saw some of the first cross-racial appointments in the conference. He earned a reputation as a unifier, someone who could work with people regardless of race. In 1993, Governor Carroll Campbell awarded him the Order of the Palmetto, the state's highest honor, for his work in uniting people. Of special note was his work to ease tensions when an integrated Methodist youth group was denied entrance to a swim club in the state.

On the evening of November 23, 1992, an assailant stabbed the bishop outside of the United Methodist Center on Colonial Drive. The stabbing occurred shortly after the death of his wife, Shirley. Bethea made a remarkable recovery from his abdominal wounds, returning to preside over the 1993 and 1994 sessions of the annual conference. His death in March 1995 of an apparent heart attack shocked the conference. More than a thousand mourners from around the Southeast attended his funeral.

"We are richer because he was here, and we are poorer because we will no longer see him in the flesh," said Bishop Woodie White.

# Chapter 6
## Bishop William Capers: A Complicated Life

Bishop William Capers played a significant role in the early history of Methodism in South Carolina and was one of the leading voices in the division of the Methodist Church in 1844. His life tells us something of the hardships and struggles of the itinerant life before the Civil War.

As the first South Carolina Methodist elected to the episcopacy, Capers wore several hats over the years. Teacher, editor, pastor, missionary, and leader of the group that helped split Methodism over slavery in the 1840s, Capers led a complicated and influential life.

Born in 1790 in St. Thomas Parish, Berkeley County, South Carolina, Capers grew up in the rice lands of Georgetown County. He studied for a time at South Carolina College, leaving to study law privately with an attorney. No doubt his studies and his legal training would help him years later, but his attendance at a camp meeting brought this son of the Lowcountry into the Methodist Church.

Capers remembered attending several early nineteenth-century camp meetings, witnessing those in attendance react powerfully to the frontier-style preaching. He joined the Methodist Episcopal Church in 1808, and while traveling the Santee Circuit with Rev. William Gassaway, at a camp meeting at Knight's Meeting House on Fork Creek, he felt a call to the ministry. Within a few months, the eighteen-year-old Capers was licensed to preach and recommended for admission to the conference, which he joined in December 1808.

Capers was ordained elder in 1812 at Bethel, Charleston, by Bishop William McKendree and appointed to Wilmington. He then served in Charleston, Orangeburg, and Columbia, South Carolina, and in Savannah and Milledgeville, Georgia, before becoming a missionary in the conference "and to the Indians," giving him a taste of nineteenth-century mission work. In 1825, he became editor of the *Wesleyan Journal*, the first attempt at a conference newspaper. He was named the presiding elder of the Charleston District in 1827, before he was forty.

Capers had grown up surrounded by slavery and was himself a slaveholder, which by 1828 was becoming more controversial in the North. While he was being considered as the American representative to the British Methodist Conference, one of the bishops told him privately that he preferred someone else because Capers owned slaves. However, the other bishops insisted, and Capers was chosen. He sailed for England in June 1828, visiting Liverpool and London and spending time with most of the great British Methodist leaders. The conference itself lasted from July 30 to August 18. His biographer notes the British had warm feelings for Capers partly because of his social graces and partly because some of the stronger anti-slavery movements in Britain were a few years in the future. In total, the trip kept Capers away from Charleston for six months.

On his return to South Carolina, Capers became superintendent of the missions to the slaves in the Lowcountry. Several planters visited him, inquiring about the Methodist Church's willingness to minister to the enslaved persons on their plantations. Capers was not interested in undertaking these duties himself but promised to find someone to serve. It must be said that the missionaries were at best paternalistic in their attitudes, and Capers himself wrote in 1836, "We regard the question of the abolition of slavery as a civil one … and not a religious one at all … ." He also wrote, "We believe that the Holy Scriptures … do unequivocally authorize the relation of master and slave."

In the 1830s, his influence continued to grow. He was offered professorships in several colleges, but he declined them all to remain in the pulpit ministry. In 1837, he became the founding editor of the *Southern Christian Advocate*. In 1841, he became the southern Missionary Secretary for the Methodist Episcopal Church, a position he held for four years.

It should therefore come as no surprise that as a delegate to the 1844 General Conference, Capers was acknowledged as a leader in the faction that defended Bishop James O. Andrew on the question of slavery. His speeches were, in the words of a historian of the day, "a vindication of the Southern view of the question." When the southern conferences withdrew from the Methodist Episcopal Church, he joined them, and in 1846, he was elected as a bishop in the Methodist Episcopal Church, South. He and Robert Paine were the first two bishops elected by the new denomination, and they were consecrated by bishops Andrew and Soule, who had been elected before the separation and who had chosen to adhere to the southern wing of the church.

Capers served throughout the region for eight years. Since the church had only four bishops and nineteen annual conferences, that kept each of the bishops busy traveling. In his first year, he visited the Virginia, Holston, North Carolina, South Carolina, Georgia, and Florida conferences, which took him from October to February. In his second year, he traveled to the west to hold conferences in Missouri, Arkansas, Indian Territory, and Texas. This also required several months of arduous travel.

The life and work of a bishop took its toll on Capers, and just days after his return to his home from presiding over the Florida Conference, he took ill and died in 1855, three days past his sixty-fifth birthday.

He did not live to see the nation divided in the way the church had split.

# Chapter 7
## Bishop Roy C. Clark

South Carolina Methodists anticipated they would be welcoming a new bishop in the summer of 1980. Bishop Edward L. Tullis had served the normal two quadrennia in Columbia, and the Jurisdictional Conference sent the Kentucky native to the Tennessee Conference. In his place, the jurisdiction sent newly elected Bishop Roy C. Clark.

Born in Mobile, Alabama, in 1920, Clark grew up in parsonages in Mississippi, where his father was a pastor. He graduated from Millsaps College and Yale Divinity School and served appointments in Mississippi. At age thirty-three, he had become pastor of Capitol Street Church in Jackson, where he served for ten years. In 1963, he moved to Memphis, serving St. John's Church, and in 1967, he began a thirteen-year pastorate at Nashville's West End United Methodist Church. He became a member of the Tennessee Conference and represented that conference at General and Jurisdictional Conference.

In 1980, the Southeastern Jurisdiction elected Clark to the episcopacy on the sixteenth ballot. He was the only minister elected that year who had not been a district superintendent and the only one who was not a conference nominee. Several other candidates that year, including Joseph Bethea, were elected in subsequent years.

The Clarks took up their responsibilities in Columbia in September 1980, and the bishop was formally installed in a service in October at Washington Street Church.

Clark noted in one article that he was not the "South Carolina bishop," but was "the United Methodist bishop assigned to South Carolina," and was already learning to balance his responsibilities to both South Carolina and to the general church. In 1982, Clark hosted the Council of Bishops for a weeklong meeting. They were unable to meet as hoped in Charleston for lack of a facility to accommodate them, so they had to meet at Lake Junaluska. Clark was determined to bring them to South Carolina, however, so the bishops came to Spartanburg for a day, where they met at Bethel Church.

Arriving only eight years after the merger of the 1785 and 1866 conferences, Clark had to continue efforts to bring about a more intentional merger. In 1984, he issued a pastoral letter outlining plans for more dialogue between White and Black Methodists, many of whom had few relationships outside of conference and district work. The letter also outlined plans for consultation regarding cross-racial pastoral appointments in future years.

Clark also faced concerns from some lay Methodists about perceived liberalism in the denomination as a whole. One newspaper article talked about a meeting he had with a Union County church that had complained about some of the church's stands on social issues. Clark responded that "liberal and conservative are not kingdom categories," and that regarding the Bible, "Interpretations disagree, but our dialogue centers around the Bible." The issues Clark faced in dealing with some of the laity show that some things don't change very much.

As he prepared to retire in 1988, in an interview with the *Advocate*, Clark noted that part of his mission in South Carolina had been to foster a sense of community. He noted that part of that was continuing the "journey of inclusiveness that we began at merger." Another part was trying to connect the local church to the annual conference, so that local church members saw themselves as part of a larger denominational mission. Clark, who spent his entire ministry in the local church, admitted that it took him a while to adjust to his new role as a bishop, whereas he expected his successor, Bishop Joseph Bethea, who had been a district superintendent and an assistant to a bishop, would know the questions to ask.

The Clarks returned to Nashville, where he served as a bishop in residence at West End Church, did some teaching at Vanderbilt, and lived until 2014.

# Chapter 8
## Bishop Collins Denny

Bishop Collins Denny was one of the leading bishops of the Methodist Episcopal Church, South, but so strongly opposed reunification that he never recognized the legitimacy of the post-reunification Methodist Church.

Born in 1854 in Winchester, Virginia, Denny studied at Princeton, then attended law school at the University of Virginia. After a few years of practicing law in Baltimore, he decided to enter the ministry. He joined the old Baltimore Annual Conference of the Methodist Episcopal Church, South, in 1880.

He served appointments in Virginia, Maryland, and West Virginia until 1891. From 1889-1891 he was the chaplain of the University of Virginia. In 1891, he accepted a position teaching mental and moral philosophy at Vanderbilt. He remained there for the next nineteen years. As a scholar, he contributed to the *Methodist Quarterly Review*, to the *Library of Southern Literature*, and other publications. Later in life, Douglas Southall Freeman, the author of the extensive biography of Robert E. Lee, asked Denny to proofread and fact-check the entire manuscript before it was published.

He was a delegate to five General Conferences, from 1894 to 1910, and was the secretary of the 1894 General Conference. No doubt his scholarly activities led him to serve on the church's book committee, which he chaired from 1898 until he became a bishop.

In 1910, the General Conference elected him to the episcopacy, where he served for the next twenty-four years. In 1913-1915, and again in 1922-1925, he presided over the South Carolina and Upper South Carolina conferences. His precision both as a scholar and a presiding officer, however, gave him a reputation as being chilly. He was exacting about the rules and would often correct clergy from the chair when they made an error of grammar or fact. That probably did not endear him to the ministers in the annual conferences where he presided.

When he was elected a bishop, he left Vanderbilt, though that was the time that Vanderbilt was in the process of leaving the denomination. He lived in Richmond for the rest of his life, traveling to meet the various annual conferences where he was assigned to preside.

Some observers claimed that Denny was the best parliamentarian the denomination ever had. One biography noted that he spent much of his time answering questions about church law and procedure. He was the secretary of the College of Bishops for seventeen years and edited six editions of the Book of Discipline of the southern church. No doubt his legal training influenced his work in the church.

He used his knowledge of law and history in his later years to oppose the reunification of the church. He retired in 1934, around his eightieth birthday, and after reunification in 1939, refused to accept his pension as a retired bishop from The Methodist Church. He and his son, who was also an attorney, sued for the right to use the name of the Methodist Episcopal Church, South. They lost. His son continued to represent opponents of desegregation in Virginia after Denny's death in 1943.

# Chapter 9
## Bishop William Wallace Duncan

As one of South Carolina's contributions to the Methodist episcopacy, William Wallace Duncan spent much of his life serving the Methodist Church.

When his father, David Duncan, joined the original Wofford College faculty in 1854, the fifteen-year-old future bishop transferred from Randolph-Macon College, where the elder Duncan had been teaching. Graduating from Wofford in 1858, Duncan returned to Virginia and entered the Methodist ministry. He served churches in Virginia for sixteen years and was also a Confederate chaplain.

Duncan returned to Wofford in January 1876 as professor of mental and moral philosophy, and he took on the additional duty of being the college's financial agent, or chief fundraiser. Over the next ten years, Duncan traveled throughout South Carolina, speaking to Methodist churches in an attempt to increase the college's endowment. Duncan was active in Methodist circles, representing South Carolina in three successive General Conferences. In 1881, he represented the Methodist Episcopal Church, South, at the first Methodist Ecumenical Conference in London. His work on Wofford's behalf brought him increased attention throughout the region, and as a result, the 1886 General Conference elected him a bishop.

His election to the episcopacy meant he had to resign from the Wofford faculty, but it did not end his relationship with the college. He became a member of the Wofford Board of Trustees, and for the last nineteen years of his life, served as the board chair. When the trustees elected Henry Nelson Snyder as the college's fourth president, Duncan presented Snyder as president of "our" college, with emphasis, Snyder later remembered, on the word "our."

Snyder later wrote of Duncan, "He looked more like a bishop than any other man I have ever known."

In those days, the denomination had more annual conferences than bishops, so the bishops presided over multiple annual conferences each year. They did not always preside over the same conference in consecutive years, either. As such, Duncan visited several different annual conferences across the South, and even had to travel to the west coast as he presided over the Oregon Annual Conference six times. When opening one annual conference, Duncan reportedly said, "I am glad to meet and greet you. I expect to be glad all the time I am with you, and possibly I may be glad when I leave you."

Conferences did not provide residences for the bishops, so Duncan chose to remain in Spartanburg. Around 1885, he started building a large home midway between the Wofford campus and downtown Spartanburg. When he became a bishop, he altered the plans to accommodate many of the large meetings he expected to host. The house was the first in the city to have inside bathrooms with running water. Wofford's literary magazine reported in February 1889 that "Bishop Duncan's handsome residence on North Church Street, second lot from the [Central] Methodist Church, is completed. It is of English architecture with coat of arms on front. The bishop has been spending some time at home."

North Church Street in Spartanburg must have been one of the most Methodist streets in the country in those days, as it included Central Methodist Church, Central's parsonage, the Spartanburg District parsonage, the bishop's residence, and Wofford. You almost have to feel a little sorry for Central's ministers, with their bishop and presiding elder living on their block. From his home, Duncan could keep an eye on events at Wofford while he handled his responsibilities to the far-flung conferences he was serving.

The home remained in the bishop's family after his death in 1908. In 1999, it was moved to make way for Spartanburg's Marriott. The house now sits on a site between the city's Magnolia Cemetery and the Carolinas campus of the Edward Via College of Osteopathic Medicine, which has beautifully restored it.

# Chapter 10
## Bishop Paul Hardin Jr.

When the 1960 Southeastern Jurisdictional Conference finished its work, South Carolina found that two of its natives had been elected bishops. In an even more interesting twist, one of those was assigned to be the first bishop of the newly created Columbia Area: Bishop Paul Hardin Jr.

Hardin was a native of Chester, South Carolina, and a 1924 Wofford graduate. He had continued his studies at Emory, and after graduating, he had joined the Western North Carolina Conference. For twenty-two years, he served appointments in Concord, Waynesville, Wadesboro, Asheboro, and Shelby, North Carolina. Wesley Memorial in High Point, North Carolina, was his last Western North Carolina church, for in 1949, he moved to Birmingham's First Methodist Church. From that church, he was elected to the episcopacy eleven years later.

Hardin wrote that he was "genuinely delighted" to return to his native state as a bishop, for he had never expected to become a bishop, nor had he expected to be assigned to the Columbia Area. He almost immediately began a weekly tradition of writing an *Advocate* column, like what he had written in his church's newsletter. It was generally a short piece, often a bunch of sentences or thoughts separated by dashes. Those columns talked about upcoming events in the conference, his travels and work with the general church, places he was visiting within the state, and his thoughts on church and world issues.

Hardin had barely been in South Carolina for six months when the death of Alabama's bishop caused his own appointment to change. The College of Bishops asked Hardin to supervise the Alabama-West Florida Conference for the remaining three years. Hardin wrote in the *Advocate* that this would cause a "drastic rearrangement" of his duties in the Palmetto State. And indeed, this turn of events, coming as it did during the most tension-filled days of the civil rights movement, put Hardin in the middle of historic change.

In April 1963, he joined with other religious leaders in Alabama in calling for Dr. Martin Luther King Jr. to slow down the movement and in calling the demonstrations in King's Birmingham campaign "unwise and untimely." Hardin and most of the other signers of the letter considered themselves supporters of desegregation and the principles of equality but were concerned the movement was going too fast. Their letter prompted Dr. King to issue his famous "Letter from Birmingham Jail." And as a result, Hardin was one of the named clergy recipients of the letter.

While this caused some of the clergy to feel embittered, Hardin responded positively and continued to lead South Carolina's Methodists toward desegregation. He had the longest tenure of any bishop to preside over the South Carolina Conference until 2012, serving for twelve years. They were indeed tumultuous years, as he had to gently but firmly steer South Carolina Methodists toward the merger of the White and Black conferences. That fact probably explains why he was returned to the state for a third quadrennium, because his knowledge of the situation made it essential that he lead the final steps of the merger.

In 1968, with the merger of the Evangelical United Brethren and the Methodist Church to form The United Methodist Church, the racially segregated Central Jurisdiction was formally abolished. The United Methodist Church essentially decreed that segregated annual conferences needed to end. With the abolition of the Central Jurisdiction, South Carolina's Central Jurisdiction Conference became part of the Southeastern Jurisdiction, and Hardin became that conference's bishop as well. Between 1968 and 1972, Hardin guided South Carolina's Black and White Methodists through merger, presiding over many special and joint sessions of annual conferences, overcoming setbacks and resistance repeatedly. At times each conference rejected merger plans.

Finally, on June 5, 1972, Hardin presided over a worship service to formally merge the two conferences. In his final report to the Southeastern Jurisdiction, Hardin noted the times he had needed to go to court to enforce the denomination's rights related to church property. He lamented that he had not wanted to do it, but knew it was necessary to defend the trust clause. He explained he felt like the church needed to do a better job educating members on the reasons behind the itinerancy.

Following his service as president of the Council of Bishops in 1971-1972, Hardin retired in July 1972 but remained active in Methodist circles until his death in 1996.

# Chapter 11
## Bishop John C. Kilgo: Bishop and Teacher

John Carlisle Kilgo has been called South Carolina Methodism's gift to North Carolina. His service to the church and to higher education in the two Carolinas makes him one of the most significant figures in the early twentieth-century church.

Born in Laurens, South Carolina, in 1861, Kilgo was the son of a Methodist minister. He grew up in Methodist parsonages all around South Carolina. He followed his older brother to Wofford College in October 1880 but stayed only through his sophomore year. His eyes were weak and caused him trouble in his studies.

He entered the ministry, being admitted to the South Carolina Conference in December 1882. Appointed to Bennettsville for 1883, he also served in Timmonsville, Rock Hill, and the Little Rock Circuit before returning to Wofford in 1889. His gifts in the pulpit brought him to the attention of the college's trustees, and he was selected to be Wofford's financial agent.

The financial agent was the chief fundraiser for the college, and thus Kilgo made extensive use of his church connections to help solicit gifts for Wofford. His two brothers, both of whom had earned Wofford degrees, had followed him into the ministry. Now that he was back at Wofford, he resumed his studies, and though he never earned a bachelor's degree, he undertook coursework privately with Dr. Henry Nelson Snyder, then a member of the English faculty. As a result, in 1892 he was granted an honorary Master of Arts—an unusual award. He also began to teach courses as a professor of metaphysics. At thirty-one, he was a popular, if brash, young professor, and rumor had it that he aspired to Wofford's presidency, which some saw as an affront to the older and highly regarded president, Dr. James H. Carlisle. He continued his work as the financial agent, representing the college at gatherings around the state.

Kilgo was destined for greater things. Only two years later, in 1894, the young minister was elected president of Trinity College, which had only recently moved to Durham, North Carolina. Trinity, in fact, was in debt at the time, and Washington Duke, who had helped bring the college to Durham, lamented that he had ever become involved with the place. Touring the campus with Kilgo, Duke reportedly said, "Well, there it is. I never expect to give another dollar to it, and I wish I had never put a dollar in it."

Kilgo presided over Trinity for sixteen years, guiding the college and repairing the institution's relationship with the Duke family. Kilgo inspired the family to resume its support, and he articulated a vision for the college. As its president, Kilgo declared that Trinity would help form opinion and not follow it. He supported industrial development in the South and was not shy about pointing out the region's social problems. Most notably, Kilgo took a liberal position on race relations, at least for the 1890s and early 1900s. He was also a strong defender of academic freedom at Trinity, and in one case, told the trustees he would rather teach ten students who believed in truth and tolerance than to teach a thousand "who believed in intolerance and regarded intellectual bondage a commendable virtue." The trustees backed Kilgo's position and, in 1903, issued a strong statement in support of academic freedom.

Kilgo was elected bishop by the 1910 General Conference, but he left Trinity well on its way to being transformed into Duke University.

As a bishop, Kilgo served throughout the denomination, presiding over sessions of the South Carolina Conference in 1911 and 1912. He had the good fortune of presiding over one annual conference in Bennettsville, the town where he had his start in the ministry thirty years earlier. He once noted that he had never wanted to be anything but a Methodist preacher, and now he could "do anything in it from holding a meeting to presiding over an annual conference."

As a bishop, he continued his advocacy for education. His abilities as a pulpit orator meant he was in great demand as a revival preacher, and he relished the task of saving souls. He served for a dozen years in the episcopacy, working until his death in 1922.

As an educator, minister, and bishop, Kilgo believed in the importance and power of Christian education.

# Chapter 12
## Bishop Edwin D. Mouzon

One of the South Carolina Conference's contributions to the episcopacy, Edwin Dubose Mouzon served more than a quarter-century as a Methodist bishop. He was a writer, an educational leader, and an advocate for church union.

Born in Spartanburg, South Carolina, and raised in that city's Central Methodist Church, Mouzon attended Wofford College in the 1880s. He graduated in 1889, one of an impressive class of sixteen that also included future Duke University President William Preston Few and United States Senator E. D. Smith. The year before he graduated from Wofford, he received his license to preach at Central Church and joined the South Carolina Conference the next fall. He was immediately transferred by Bishop William Wallace Duncan to the Texas Conference, where he spent most of the next twenty years of his ministry. He also spent three years at Central Methodist Church in Kansas City before returning to serve the Travis Park Church in San Antonio, Texas, then the largest congregation in the West Texas Conference. In 1908, he took a professorship in theology at Southwestern University in Georgetown, Texas, and in 1910, the General Conference elected him as a bishop.

The new bishop was only forty-one years old.

In his years as a bishop, Mouzon presided over annual conferences in Texas, Colorado, New Mexico, Mississippi, Montana, the Carolinas, California, and Virginia, and he even led missions to East Asia, Mexico, and South America. He helped set up the autonomous Methodist Church of Brazil, attended various ecumenical conferences, and chaired several significant movements in the life of the church. As a presiding officer, an observer noted, he had the admirable qualities of never making hasty decisions, being sensitive to the needs of his ministers, and never speaking a bitter word toward any who disagreed with him.

Mouzon's particular interest was in higher education, and he helped found Southern Methodist University. In 1915, he helped found the Perkins School of Theology at SMU, serving as its acting dean for a time. As a trustee of Scarritt College, he helped move it from Kansas City to Nashville. He chaired the General Board of Christian Education as well.

Perhaps even more importantly, he was a leader in the movement to unify the northern and southern branches of the Methodist Episcopal Church. As the chairman of the Commission on Church Union, he worked past the failure of reunification in the 1920s. When the attempt failed in 1925, he wrote to one of the northern bishops, "We will not stop. The unification of our two churches must be. The men who are vociferous today cannot speak the word tomorrow .… So long as I live, I will plead this cause."

He did not live to see unification in 1939, but he laid much of the groundwork for it.

In addition to his episcopal duties, he wrote several books. *Does God Care?* and *Fundamentals of Methodism* were two of them. Three others were the published lecture series he gave at Southern Methodist, Vanderbilt, and Yale, respectively. The latter was titled *Preaching with Authority* and was presented as the Lyman Beecher Lectures on Preaching for 1929.

In January 1937, he returned to his roots in Spartanburg to preach the centennial anniversary sermon at Central Church, where he was introduced by his friend and collaborator on church union, Dr. Henry Nelson Snyder, Wofford's longtime president. He reminded his audience that Central was the only church where he had ever been a member.

Snyder later wrote that Mouzon must have deeply felt the presence of the great cloud of witnesses surrounding him and the congregation at Central that day, recognizing how much of that church he had taken out into his ministry.

A month later, while sitting in his home in Charlotte talking with a colleague about the Bishop's Crusade, he died. He had been the senior bishop in the southern church and had been a leading voice in promoting education and union.

# Chapter 13
## Bishop A. Coke Smith

Alexander Coke Smith was another of South Carolina Methodism's contributions to the episcopacy.

Born in Lynchburg, South Carolina, Coke Smith enrolled at Wofford in 1868 and graduated in 1872. His father was a Methodist minister, so he grew up in parsonages around the state. After graduating from Wofford, he joined the South Carolina Conference and was sent to his first appointment, Cheraw Station. After a year there, he went to Columbia to serve that city's Washington Street Church, where he remained three years. Smith was the junior preacher in his first year and the pastor in charge the second and third years—at the ripe old age of twenty-six. Next, he went to Greenville Station—Buncombe Street Church—in 1876, serving for four years. Continuing his journeys around the state, the young minister went to serve Trinity, Charleston, for three years, from 1880-1982, where he became close to Bishop William M. Wightman in the older man's last years.

Smith then spent four years, 1883-1886, as the presiding elder of the Columbia District, and following that, was elected to the professorship of mental and moral philosophy at Wofford. He followed in the footsteps of William Wallace Duncan, who had just been elected a bishop. That chair on the Wofford faculty actually produced three bishops: Duncan, Smith, and Smith's successor, John C. Kilgo. Additionally, that faculty position was responsible for fundraising, so it gave Smith the opportunity to travel around South Carolina, representing Wofford, preaching in various pulpits, and making stronger personal connections.

Though a young man, Smith sometimes suffered under the strain of his workload. Wofford historian David Duncan Wallace noted that "he had just almost killed himself saving souls in one of the greatest revivals in the history of Charleston," and proceeded to conclude the process by his labors for raising the college endowment.

After four years at Wofford, he was elected to the 1890 General Conference, heading the South Carolina delegation. He was just forty-one years old. The General Conference elected him as one of their three missionary secretaries, but he only stayed in this position for a few months before he was asked to become professor of practical theology at Vanderbilt. He moved again in 1892, transferring his membership to the Virginia Conference and serving churches there until 1902. He came close to being elected a bishop in 1898 and was elected to the episcopacy in 1902.

He died in December 1906 in Asheville, having served a relatively short tenure as a bishop. Collins Denny, himself later a bishop, noted that Smith was "a man of rare versatility and adaptability, and charmed every circle and community into which he entered. He was a past master in delicate humor, and this gift was his servant, never his master." His Methodist education had served him well, for "he had read widely and well, and his tenacious memory gave him ready command of his resources."

Bishops often need a blend of skills, and from what his contemporaries wrote, Smith brought a mix of political acumen, intelligence, and preaching ability to that office.

# Chapter 14
## Bishop John Owen Smith

When John Owen Smith was elected a bishop in July 1960, he became the first member of the South Carolina Conference to be elevated to the episcopacy in more than half a century. With as many talented clergy as the South Carolina Conference produced in the years around and after World War II, he must have been an especially talented minister.

Born in Edgefield County, South Carolina, in 1902, Smith grew up in the town of Johnston, and attended Harmony Methodist Church. After graduating from the local high school, he enrolled at Wofford in 1918. He studied there for four years, earning distinctions in scholarship and graduating in 1922. While at Wofford, he gained some experience in leadership as the president of the sophomore class. He also was the manager of the Glee Club, served in numerous offices in the Carlisle Literary Society, and was the assistant advertising manager for the college yearbook. Following graduation from Wofford, he journeyed north to attend Yale Divinity School, graduating with his Bachelor of Divinity in 1925. He joined the Upper South Carolina Conference, where he was ordained deacon in 1927 and elder in 1929.

The young minister served his early years in Leesville, then spent most of the 1930s at Clemson and Laurens. He went on to serve several large historic churches between 1938 and 1954, including Washington Street in Columbia, Buncombe Street in Greenville, and Central in Spartanburg. In 1954, he was named Spartanburg District Superintendent, where he oversaw the growth of new churches in Spartanburg's suburbs.

Wofford honored him in several significant ways. In 1941, he became an alumnus member of Phi Beta Kappa, and in 1946, he received an honorary

Doctor of Divinity. He was the featured speaker at the Wofford alumni banquet during Commencement 1943. In 1944, he presented the historical address at annual conference, speaking about the history of Epworth Children's Home. He wrote more than a few pieces in the Advocate over the years.

He was elected to General Conferences in 1948, 1952, 1956, and 1960. Newspaper reports indicated that in 1956, he was touted as an episcopal candidate, though he was not elected. He had certainly made a name for himself as a member of the General Board of Education, as the president of the Southeastern Jurisdiction's ministerial group, and as a vice president of the district superintendents of the jurisdiction. He was clearly an intellectual and someone other clergy looked to for leadership.

His tenure as a district superintendent ended at the 1960 Annual Conference, and he was appointed to Bethel, Charleston. Thus, he served at the old historic church in each of South Carolina's four largest cities of that era.

His service at Bethel was short, for the 1960 Southeastern Jurisdictional Conference elected him a bishop and assigned him to the Atlanta area. He served the North Georgia and South Georgia conferences for twelve years, helping shepherd Georgia's Methodist congregations through the era of desegregation. He was elected at the same jurisdictional conference as South Carolina native and fellow Wofford alumnus Paul Hardin Jr., who was then serving in Alabama and who returned to the Columbia area.

Smith retired in 1972, taught at Emory, and was elected an honorary member of the South Carolina Conference in 1977. Following his death in 1978, he was buried at Harmony Methodist Church, where he had received his call to preach and preached his first sermon.

# Chapter 15
## Bishop James S. Thomas

Bishop James S. Thomas was one of South Carolina's most significant contributions to The United Methodist Church. His pioneering work helped lead to the end of racial segregation in the church's hierarchy.

Thomas was born on April 9, 1919, in Orangeburg. His father, the Reverend James S. Thomas Sr., was a clergyman serving there.

Thomas enrolled at Claflin University, graduating in 1939 with a degree in sociology. He first became an educator, spending a year as a school principal in Florence County. However, he could not ignore his call to the ministry, and he was ordained deacon and elder in subsequent years. He attended Gammon Theological Seminary and served the Orangeburg Circuit. He went on to earn a master's degree at Drew University.

Back in South Carolina, he served two years on the York Circuit and was also a chaplain at South Carolina State College. From the local church, Thomas found a calling in higher education, going on to become a professor at Gammon Seminary. While there, he earned his PhD in sociology and anthropology at Cornell University. During part of his time at Gammon, he served as acting president of the seminary.

In 1953, he took a position as associate general secretary of the Methodist General Board of Education, with responsibilities for assisting and supporting the denomination's historically black colleges. He served at the General Board for a dozen years, retaining his clergy membership in the South Carolina 1866 Conference.

We sometimes act as though the modern civil rights movement suddenly emerged from thin air in 1954. Nothing could be further from the truth, and many Black Methodist clergy were leaders in the movement to end segregation in our society and in our church. During the 1950s, many Methodists began to question the bargain that had been negotiated during the 1939 reunification of the northern and southern branches of Methodism, the bargain that relegated African-American Methodists into the segregated Central Jurisdiction. As early as 1952, the General Conference had said "there is no place for racial discrimination or segregation in the Methodist Church." The very existence of the South Carolina Conference (1866) proved these to be empty words, and the conference, in 1955, said as much. Thomas was at the forefront of the long, slow campaign to dismantle segregation in the church.

Though the Central Jurisdiction still existed in 1964, Thomas was elected to the episcopacy by the North Central Jurisdiction, becoming the youngest Methodist bishop at the time of his election. He was assigned to the Iowa Area, one of the largest annual conferences in the denomination, where he served until 1976. During those twelve years, the merger with the Evangelical United Brethren Church created The United Methodist Church, the Central Jurisdiction was abolished, and former Black conferences throughout the country merged into integrated conferences.

Thomas eventually became president of the Council of Bishops, served as chair of the Social Principles Study Commission, and delivered the principal episcopal address in 1976.

Claflin remained dear to his heart, and he helped the university raise funds on numerous occasions. A longtime trustee, he chaired the board and was inducted into the Claflin Hall of Fame. He also received honors from colleges across the Midwest, including Ohio Wesleyan, Iowa Wesleyan, and DePauw. In South Carolina, both Claflin and Wofford conferred honorary doctorates on him.

In 1972, he became the first African American to receive an honorary degree from Wofford.

In 1976, he was assigned to the East Ohio Conference, where he served until retirement in 1988. He continued his ministry as a bishop-in-residence at Emory and at Clark Atlanta and continued his work of mentoring and teaching until his death in 2010 at age ninety-one.

# Chapter 16
## Bishop Edward L. Tullis

In July 1972, South Carolina Methodists were anticipating the arrival of a new bishop. Their leader for the previous twelve years, Bishop Paul Hardin Jr., was retiring, and changes were definitely coming. Hardin had patiently guided the merger of the former 1785 and 1866 conferences, but the real work of merging was in the future and would be led by someone else.

In July, the Southeastern Jurisdiction elected six new bishops. Two elections occurred on the first two ballots, and a third occurred on the sixth ballot. The conference struggled along for several ballots until, on the fourteenth ballot, Edward Lewis Tullis of Kentucky was elected.

Bishop Tullis had been running in about fourth place on earlier ballots, but as often happens in episcopal elections, he gradually rose and finally earned the required margin on July 14. South Carolinians soon learned he would be assigned to the Columbia Area.

Tullis was born in Cincinnati in 1917 but had lived his whole life in Kentucky. He was a 1939 graduate of Kentucky Wesleyan and had his seminary degree from Louisville Presbyterian Seminary. He had spent his entire ministry in Kentucky, serving as the minister at First Church in Ashland since 1961. Before that, he had served as an associate at Fourth Avenue Church in Louisville and as pastor of First Church in Frankfort for nine years, where he had also been a chaplain for the Kentucky legislature. He had been elected to represent Kentucky at General Conference five times since 1956 and became the first Kentuckian elected bishop in more than one hundred years.

The transition moved quickly. Bishop and Mrs. Tullis returned to Ashland, where he preached his last service on July 23. Later that day, they flew to Columbia, where he assumed some of his responsibilities on July 24. After a hectic week of moving, the new bishop left for a conference of district superintendents at Lake Junaluska, where he met with the South Carolina Cabinet. He later noted that he really had no expectation of being elected bishop, and indeed, he had never even been a district superintendent.

The new bishop already had a called session of the annual conference on his schedule. As part of the merger, the conference had scheduled an adjourned session for October 1972 to elect members of the various committees of the merged conference. The merger would require all the new bishop's political and pastoral skills. The conference's elections reflected the diversity of the new conference, but when those boards met to organize and elect officers, none of them elected a Black chairperson. With the guidance of the bishop and the Committee on Merger, the conference voted to require each board to meet within thirty days to organize to try to be certain that members of both former conferences had opportunities for leadership, and those committees all took that guidance to heart.

Tullis served eight years in Columbia, and one of the historians of the conference noted how hard he worked to build relationships with the Black clergy and their families. Many noted that he made the effort to learn all their names and build trust where there was none. The bishop was also an advocate of women in the clergy and ordained the first women to be admitted to the South Carolina Conference. One newspaper article said that while hearing a national news anchor claim the Episcopal Church was becoming the first American church to ordain women, he called the network on the phone immediately and was put through to the newsman before the broadcast was over to correct him.

After leaving Columbia, Tullis went to Nashville for four years before retiring in 1984. He and his wife, Mary Jane, retired to Lake Junaluska, where he taught a Sunday school class for the next twenty years. He died in 2005.

## Chapter 17
### Bishop William M. Wightman

Few members of our annual conference today can claim to have had as varied a ministry as the Reverend William May Wightman, whose service touched several important areas of Methodist life in South Carolina.

Born in Charleston, South Carolina, on January 29, 1808, Wightman grew up in that city's Trinity Church. His mother, who was a native of Plymouth, England, came from an old British Methodist family, and family legend says she sat on John Wesley's lap as a small child. William Wightman was a member of the first Sunday school established in the Holy City, and at a camp meeting in 1826, after hearing the preaching of future bishop James Andrew, had his conversion experience.

At nineteen, Wightman graduated first in his class at the College of Charleston and on his twentieth birthday was admitted to the South Carolina Conference. In the late 1820s and 1830s, he served churches on the Pee Dee Circuit and in Orangeburg, Charleston, Santee, and Camden. In 1833, he ventured into the Upcountry, serving in Abbeville, and then from 1834 to 1838, he served as financial agent for, and then professor at, Randolph Macon College in Virginia. His work at Randolph Macon, which was essentially the only Methodist college in the South, put him in contact with many influential educators and supporters in the church, likely including Benjamin Wofford. Thus, in his first ten years of ministry, he had served in the pulpit, as a fundraiser, and as a professor.

After five successful years there, he returned to become presiding elder of the Cokesbury District (at age thirty-one) and then in 1841, was named editor of the Charleston-based *Southern Christian Advocate*. He held that position for thirteen years—which was probably the longest time he was in a single place. His tenure at the helm of the *Advocate* gave him a prominent position and platform in the conference, and his words were no doubt read by most influential Methodists around the state. During the 1840s, as Methodists fought over slavery, he was one of the voices explaining what was happening in the church to South Carolinians. His first election as a delegate to the General Conference came in 1840, and he was a member of the 1844 conference that saw American Methodism split into northern and southern branches. In 1845, he represented South Carolina at the founding conference of the Methodist Episcopal Church, South. He was a delegate from South Carolina to the next four General Conferences. In 1854, he was nearly elected bishop, and would have been except for an error in a delegate's ballot. Someone wrote "William M. Bishop," and Wightman happened to be one vote short. By this point, he was generally recognized as the leading clergy member of the South Carolina Conference.

That mistake may have been beneficial for Wofford College. Benjamin Wofford's will named Wightman as a founding trustee in 1851, and the trustees elected him to be the chair. As the college was being built, his fellow trustees had elected him president in 1853. Thus, the pastor, fundraiser, presiding elder, professor, and editor took on the role of college president. For five years, he helped get Wofford on a firm footing, and then in 1859, the fledgling Southern University in Alabama called him to its presidency. He remained there until 1866, when he was at last elected to the episcopacy.

Wightman made Charleston his episcopal residence. He purchased a house at 79 Anson Street in the Ansonborough section of Charleston. That house, built before 1760 and known as the Daniel Legare house, is one of the oldest homes still standing in Ansonborough. He did not automatically become the bishop of the South Carolina Conference, as the church's College of Bishops also rode the circuit, rotating the responsibilities of presiding over the various conferences. On four occasions, Wightman presided over the South Carolina Conference—including in his first two years as bishop. He also traveled extensively in the west, supervising conferences in the Southwest, Oklahoma, and other faraway places. He continued this service almost up to his death, even presiding in South Carolina for the last time in 1879.

When he died in 1882, the bells of St. Michael's tolled for him, a rare honor that the Episcopalians conferred upon this leader of southern Methodist higher education. Wightman was buried in Charleston's Magnolia Cemetery.

# Chapter 18
## Reverend James Belin

In the South Carolina Conference, we hear about the James L. Belin Trust occasionally, and we hear about Belin Memorial United Methodist Church as well. We might even speculate about how we should pronounce the name! But why are we talking about a minister who served in the antebellum era and died in 1859?

The Reverend James Lynch Belin was born in All Saints Parish, South Carolina, on the Waccamaw Neck of Georgetown District in 1788. His ancestry was French Huguenot, though like many Lowcountry Carolinians of that background, his family were Episcopalians. His family was wealthy, and thus he had better educational opportunities than most. We know very little of his life before he joined the South Carolina Annual Conference in December 1811. We know he had four sisters and no brothers, and that generally in his family and social class, when they were converted to the faith, even if by Methodist ministers, they were more likely to join the Presbyterian or Episcopal church. Methodism was looked down upon as a religion for the humble. That didn't seem to bother Belin, who was later ordained deacon and elder. From 1812 to 1818, he served several Lowcountry circuits as well as one in Georgia. However, his health started to fail by 1818, and that and the death of his father forced him to leave the itinerant ministry.

Belin married Elizabeth Laval, who was the sister of his sister's husband. While a biography of Belin and his record of appointments don't completely line up on the dates, it does appear that James and Elizabeth Belin moved to Mandarin, Florida, for a few years for his health. They stayed three years, acquiring a house, farm, and orange grove. He returned to South Carolina on account of difficulties that White settlers in Florida had with Native Americans. The Florida property eventually became the property of the Florida Conference, according to family histories. It was not part of his estate at his death. Elizabeth Belin died in 1821, and ten years later, he married Charlotte Withers, who was eleven years younger than him. Neither marriage produced any children.

Belin began the work for which he is best known, which was mission work to the enslaved persons on the Waccamaw Neck, at a young age. He preached in the 1810s at Brookgreen and Springfield plantations, with the consent of the plantation owners. He remained a local pastor until 1837, when he rejoined the South Carolina Conference and was appointed to the mission to the slaves on Waccamaw Neck. He served the Waccamaw Mission for five years, retiring again in 1842. No doubt he continued his missionary work for his remaining years.

James and Charlotte Belin spent their winters at Wachesaw Plantation and their summers on Pawleys Island. When he died after a fall from his carriage in May 1859 caused by a runaway horse, he left nearly his entire estate for mission work in the South Carolina Conference in general and the Waccamaw Neck in particular. It was a substantial estate, including lands from a rice plantation, bank and railroad stock, and several enslaved persons.

The Belin Trust continues to provide funding for missions in South Carolina.

What are we to make of James Belin? His tombstone says he was "called and chosen and faithful." He carried on a ministry to a group of people that others weren't interested in serving. However, he was also a slaveowner himself. His will instructed his executors and trustees to care for his "servants" in the same manner he had. Manumission was just about impossible in South Carolina by the 1850s, so freeing his enslaved persons before or at his death was not legally possible.

Scholars disagree on what sort of gospel the ministers to the slaves preached, and how much of the gospel the planters really wanted them to hear. Much of their focus was on obedience and rewards in the next life, and none of it was on freedom.

However, it appears Belin had a long-term vision for these men and women he ministered with, and that vision still bears fruit today.

# Chapter 19
## President James H. Carlisle

James Henry Carlisle, Wofford's most influential faculty member of the nineteenth century, was born in Winnsboro, South Carolina, on May 4, 1825. His father's family had migrated from County Antrim in Northern Ireland in 1818. All his family members are buried in the Methodist churchyard in Winnsboro, which is next door to his boyhood home.

Carlisle grew up and was educated in Winnsboro before riding off on horseback to South Carolina College in 1842. There, he joined the sophomore class and graduated in December 1844, the second honor graduate of his class. He was not part of the old upper class of the state that dominated the college in those days. He taught in the Odd Fellows Academy in Columbia and the Columbia Male Academy for several years, and in 1848, he married Mary Jane Bryce.

He was attending a meeting of the South Carolina Annual Conference in Newberry in fall 1853 when someone told him in passing that Wofford College had been organized and he had been elected professor of mathematics. This came as a surprise, for he had not sought the position. He later told friends that had he been consulted, he would have preferred being named to the chair of mental and moral philosophy.

He arrived in Spartanburg the next August, at age twenty-nine, and took up residence in the campus home where he lived for the next fifty years. Six years after coming to Spartanburg, in November 1860, he was elected to represent the county in the secession convention. He voted against secession but signed the Ordinance of Secession. The Wofford archives has a copy of a bill of sale documenting Carlisle's purchase of an older enslaved woman named Nancy in 1857, whose previous enslaver was moving away from Spartanburg, but there is no evidence that Nancy Carlisle lived in his household. She became a member of Spartanburg's Central Methodist Church and died in 1864. There is no evidence Carlisle ever owned any other enslaved persons.

Following the Civil War, some on campus feared he would be imprisoned by federal soldiers for his role in signing the Ordinance of Secession. The end of the Civil War saw the loss of Wofford's entire endowment, causing many of the professors to take on extra duties. In the late 1860s, Carlisle gave lectures on astronomy to people in Spartanburg and charged a small admission fee. He used the proceeds to purchase a telescope that is still in the college's possession.

Elected president in 1875, he declined to move into the president's home on campus. He explained that he thought the home the college had already provided for him was enough of a palace. Carlisle made the education of his students, and particularly their moral education, his top priority. Though he was officially professor of mathematics and astronomy, he really preferred to teach morals and religion. He focused the faculty's personal attention on each student, but this could only be done with a relatively small student body. Each student at some point in his time at Wofford was invited to spend the evening at Dr. Carlisle's home. It was an experience those students remembered for the rest of their lives.

The college gradually moved out of a period of financial peril, though by no means did it become a prosperous institution. Three successive financial agents, all of whom were future Methodist bishops, worked among the college's friends to replace the ruined endowment. Carlisle's own relationship with the Methodist Church was strong. He was regularly a lay member of Annual Conference, and when the Methodist Episcopal Church, South, started allowing lay representation at General Conference in 1870, he was a delegate from South Carolina to almost every quadrennial meeting. He was twice elected to the Ecumenical Conference but did not attend the 1881 meeting in London, saying that travel made him ill. His influence was felt far beyond Wofford, as he was probably the most influential layperson in South Carolina Methodism in that era.

Carlisle submitted his resignation as president to the trustees in 1901, but it was a year later before they finally accepted it and named his successor. He remained a part of the campus for seven more years, speaking in chapel and visiting with alumni who dropped by his home.

When he died on October 21, 1909, his funeral was attended by some 5,000 people, including students, alumni, ministers, and citizens throughout the state. He was one of the last links to the college's very beginning.

# Chapter 20
## President Henry Nelson Snyder

Dr. Henry Nelson Snyder served as Wofford College's fourth president from 1902 to 1942, and at the same time, was one of the leading laymen of South Carolina Methodism. He was a highly influential leader in state and national higher education circles as well as in national Methodist circles, and his was a leading voice in the movement toward Methodist reunification in 1939.

Snyder was a Tennessee native who came to Wofford and Spartanburg in 1890 to become a professor of English. He had earned his degrees at Vanderbilt, which was founded to be the central university of the Methodist Episcopal Church, South. Some of his teachers there had Wofford connections as well as deep ties to the Methodist Church. After a decade at Wofford, he did what many young American academics in the 1890s and early 1900s did: He went to a German university to study for his doctorate. He would have completed it if Wofford had not called him to the presidency while he was working on his degree

Snyder's ties to regional and national higher education movements began in the 1890s, when he was one of two Wofford professors to attend the organizational meeting of the Southern Association of Colleges and Schools, which is the regional accrediting agency for colleges and schools throughout the Southeast. He also built networks in South Carolina's fledgling public schools in the 1910s and 1920s and was on good terms with many school superintendents and principals. This helped him recruit students to attend Wofford and the other Methodist colleges in the state. He also organized summer schools for teachers at Wofford for many years. He served for a time on the state Board of Education.

Snyder's commitment was to make Wofford a first-rate Methodist-related institution and to blend academic excellence with spiritual development. He wrote that he never let himself forget the importance of the college's church relationship. It is evident that the church leadership trusted their president, for they eventually made him the chair of the conference Board of Education, which was responsible for selecting the trustees for each of the conference's colleges. That's perhaps not the best practice today, but in that place and time, it worked. Snyder helped get the Textile Industrial Institute, now Spartanburg Methodist College, off the ground, providing support to the Reverend David English Camak, his former student and the college's president, and quietly persuading Spartanburg's textile leaders and South Carolina's ambivalent Methodist leaders that the institute's mission was worthy of their support. Snyder wrote that the Annual Conference gave him a free hand in the administration of the college, and this allowed him to build a fine college and faculty over his tenure. While he occasionally had to defend the faculty from critics who objected to a modernizing curriculum, no one ever seriously threatened his independence.

The conference regularly elected Snyder as a General Conference delegate, and year after year, he served on various church boards. He was a member of the Hymnal Revision Commission that produced the 1905 and the 1935 Methodist hymnal, and for some twenty years, he was one of the southern church's members on the Reunification Commission. The 1935 hymnal was produced to be the hymnal for the entire Methodist church, even though reunification was a few years away. Snyder was a member of the reuniting General Conference in 1939 when the Methodist Church was born.

As a leader in church-related higher education, he was away from Wofford for the better part of a year in the 1920s as he worked with a church-wide educational fundraising campaign, a cause that benefited Methodist-related colleges throughout the South.

Snyder retired as Wofford's president in 1942 after a forty-year tenure but remained in his house on the campus until his death in 1949. He continued to be a leading voice in Spartanburg, in educational circles, and in Methodist circles up until his death. Throughout his life, Snyder was more than simply a liberal arts college president. He was an ambassador for education at all levels, and he was a firm believer in the important role the Methodist Church played in education.

He also played an active role in the creation of the Methodist Church, using his experiences and wisdom to help heal a century-long breach in the church.

# Chapter 21
## Maria Davies Wightman and the Woman's Missionary Society

Mrs. Maria Davies Wightman lived in several states, but she became one of the most prominent women in South Carolina Methodism as the founding president of the Woman's Missionary Society of the South Carolina Conference. Given how the organization has evolved, she stands first in the line of women to have led the conference's women's organization.

Born in 1833 in the home of her great-grandfather, a Revolutionary War veteran of the siege of Yorktown, Maria Davies moved as a small child first to Montgomery, Alabama, then to Macon, Mississippi. She graduated first in her class in 1849 from Centenary Institute in Summerfield, Alabama.

During the Civil War, her family moved to Greensboro, Alabama, where Southern University was located. A South Carolina clergyman named William Wightman was serving as the university's chancellor, having left Wofford College in 1859 to help start the new university. (This college eventually became Birmingham-Southern.) In 1862, Maria Davies met Wightman, who was a widower with five children. Despite a twenty-five-year age difference, they married in November 1863.

In 1866, the General Conference of the Methodist Episcopal Church, South, elected William Wightman a bishop, and the Wightmans moved to Charleston, Bishop Wightman's home, to establish his episcopal residence. Bishop Wightman traveled throughout the country to preside over annual conferences, and Mrs. Wightman found herself busy supporting the bishop and raising their two children.

And here began her involvement with missionary society work. For years, women in Methodism had wanted to create an official organization to coordinate the women's work already under way in the church but had been discouraged by the church hierarchy. In 1878, the Woman's Missionary Society of the Methodist Episcopal Church, South, was approved by General Conference and a constitution prepared by the College of Bishops. On May 23, 1878, the society was organized, and plans were made to establish societies in each Annual Conference. Mrs. Wightman helped organize the society and suggested each Annual Conference should also have a society.

The bishops appointed the initial officers of the church-wide society, and the eight bishops' wives became vice presidents. When the South Carolina Conference met in November 1878 in Newberry, the conference missionary secretary invited any interested women to meet to form a society for South Carolina. Mrs. Wightman was asked to preside. The nominating committee recommended her for the presidency of the conference Woman's Missionary Society, and she was elected. Some sources have suggested that she was the first woman to preside over a public meeting in the history of South Carolina.

Mrs. Wightman remained as president of the conference Woman's Missionary Society after Bishop Wightman died in 1882, and for thirty more years, until her own death in 1912. Many of the articles in her papers testify to the strength and resolve she brought to her position, for she was intent on supporting women who wanted to serve the church. When the conference society held its first annual meeting at Trinity Church, Charleston, in April 1880, she addressed the assembled members as to why they were not holding their state meeting during annual conference. "At this time, we have, all to ourselves, two days for consultation, for reports, suggestions, for united, specific, continuous prayer, and an opportunity to see our duty and our privilege, that our lives may take a deeper meaning and purpose." Had they met during conference, they would have felt like a side show.

She concluded her address, "We need faithful, willing hearts and hands for service … . I say to each of you, my sisters, your hand is wanted. The Lord has need of you."

And so, Mrs. Maria Wightman spent the next thirty years organizing the missions work of South Carolina's Methodist women.

# Chapter 22
## Mary Belle Winn, Missionary to China

Several years ago, a collection of some 147 letters arrived at the Conference Archives at Wofford. A South Carolina Methodist missionary serving in China wrote them to her family in the College Place section of Columbia. They provide a glimpse at both the life of Mary Belle Winn, the daughter of a minister in the conference, during the 1920s and 1930s, and at the challenges faced by missionaries during those turbulent years.

Winn's letters from 1923 recount her travels across the United States and the Pacific on the way to her appointment in Soochow, China. Her letters after arriving describe the various Methodist-related institutions in the city—the hospital, a settlement house, and the schools, as well as the university. She appeared to be more shocked by the living conditions outside of the mission areas. She observed that the streets were narrow and covered with filth, and the city lacked proper sewage, which was a problem in a city of close to 800,000 people. She confessed to breathing through a handkerchief at times, though she told her family she supposed she'd get used to it.

Her letters describe some of the missionaries' activities. Winn had to undertake extensive study of Chinese when she arrived, but soon she was mixing language school with teaching. She reported in November that she was rushing to get her Christmas presents for her family in the mail. After Christmas, she wrote that her packages from her family in South Carolina had yet to arrive.

Her letters are full of stories about members of the missionary community, of their work, and their travels. Some of the details are especially vivid. In the summer of 1935, as she was leaving for her furlough year in the United States, she wrote about four passengers trying to get on the ship as it was pulling away from the dock. A harbor pilot had to bring them out to the ship, which Winn found very exciting.

The missionaries attended their annual conference and missionary society meetings, and Winn once wrote of her disappointment at having her appointment changed by the bishop. Still, those meetings allowed the Americans who were in the mission field to get to know each other, and Winn reported of the many invitations she had to visit with other Methodist missionaries in different parts of China. She traveled to Shanghai frequently, and on a few occasions, she had to be evacuated there.

Especially in the later letters, Winn describes the unrest in China, and some of her letters from 1938 in Shanghai refer to the Japanese invasion of China, censorship, and the closeness of war. Fortunately, Winn did not wind up as a captive during World War II. She did return to China for a few years after the war, and about a dozen letters tell of her postwar experiences. After the Chinese Communists expelled American missionaries, Winn went on to work in the mission field in Pakistan for eight more years. Later in life, she lived at the Methodist Home in Orangeburg, later known as The Oaks, where she died in 1980.

This collection of letters, though rarely used by researchers, would be useful to someone studying church history, missionary work, twentieth-century China, women's history, or another similar topic. The stories here offer only the quickest glimpse of what's in the rest of the letters.

One purpose of the Conference Archives is to collect materials like these letters. They provide insights into the lives of those who once lived among us, and they connect us to our past. With our new space in Wofford's Sandor Teszler Library, we have a greater ability to house collections like these.

# Chapter 23
## Louise Best, Missionary to Brazil

One of the South Carolina Conference's many contributions to the Methodist Church's mission work was Miss Louise Best, who served for some thirty-seven years as an educator in Brazil.

The daughter of the Reverend Albert H. Best and Lillie Andrews Best, Louise Best grew up in a Methodist parsonage. She was born while her father was serving at Mars Bluff, South Carolina, and grew up in Clyde, Gourdine, Sumter, Greer, Campobello, Newberry, and McCormick, among other places. She attended Lander College (it was a Methodist college in those days) and Scarritt Bible and Training College in Kansas City. Scarritt was known for its work in training women for the mission field.

Best went to Brazil in the early 1920s, where she was sent, along with Miss Eunice Andrews, to help found a school in the city of Santa Maria, in the southernmost Brazilian state of Rio Grande do Sul. That part of Brazil was fairly remote and was influenced by the Gaucho culture of Argentina.

The school, Colegio Centenario, opened with seven students in March 1922. They chose that name, which in English would be Centenary College, because 1922 was the centennial of Brazilian independence. The school was largely supported by the Women's Society of Christian Service. It was originally a school for girls, and it started in a cottage. During the next thirty years, it grew to include four large buildings and encompassed a primary school, a high school, and junior college classes. For much of her time in Brazil, Best was the principal of Colegio Centenario.

Except for her first six months spent near Rio, Best spent the entirety of her thirty-seven years in the mission field in Santa Maria, Brazil. Some of her letters appeared on the Women's Society of Christian Service pages in the *Advocate*. Some of her letters speak of the vastness of Brazil's countryside—it took four days by train to get to conferences in Rio de Janeiro. Other letters speak of construction projects—building the primary school, her hopes for a chapel—and of the support the mission had received from home. In later years, she wrote of the work that the college's alumnae had undertaken to raise needed funds.

As she neared retirement, the city of Santa Maria made her an honorary citizen, which was noted as a nice honor considering how the locals were a little suspicious of this Methodist mission in its early days. By the time she retired and returned to South Carolina, Best noted, the school had as many Catholic as Protestant students.

Following her retirement in 1958, she settled in Spartanburg, where one of her younger brothers lived. She spoke regularly in churches around the conference about her life and mission work. Part of her reason for speaking was no doubt to encourage others to enter the field, for as she told a reporter, "The need for missionaries far exceeds the number making applications and this is tragic."

She was attending a reunion of a handful of missionaries at the home of a minister in North Carolina when she died in July 1966.

## One of Louise Best's letters from Brazil

My dear friends,

July 28 was a wonderful day for me. It marked the thirtieth anniversary of my arrival in Brazil. That night I gave a dinner for the members of the faculty, members of the board of trustees, our pastor and his wife, the doctors whom we call, and the school inspector. July is the month of winter school holidays in Brazil. Some of the teachers were at home but most of them were in the city.

Brazil is indeed a country of surprises! One of the greatest was an invitation to have lunch at the Rotary Club on August 1. When I arrived, I found that it was a special luncheon in honor of my thirty years in Brazil, and during that time, with the exception of six months near Rio, in Santa Maria.

Once a month our pastor leads chapel at the school. Last Thursday was the first assembly since the holidays and he was present. Before he began his talk, he said that one of the teachers had a story to tell. At the beginning I did not recognize the person about whom she was talking. When Dona Maria finished, I arose and thanked her for her kind words and assured them of my joy in being here. Imagine my surprise when the girls from the primary and high school as well as one of the teachers made speeches and gave lovely flowers. All those demonstrations of love and appreciation make me humbly grateful for these years of service in Brazil and especially at Colegio Centenario.

We are all rejoicing over the money for our primary building. We plan to break ground on September 7. I shall write you again after the ceremony.

In July I attended Central Council in São Paulo. Another good trip by air. It takes four hours by plane and four days by train.

The annual meeting of the laymen of the South Brazil Conference was held in Santa Maria in July. The delegates were entertained at the Methodist Home, but the college offered a special dinner in their honor. There were fifty present. Also in July we had the privilege of entertaining the district meeting of young people and juveniles. It was a very good conference.

August is brotherhood month among the Protestant youth of this conference. In Santa Maria each Saturday evening they have had a special meeting at the different churches in the city; on Sunday afternoons open air meetings. Last night the final service was held in the Lutheran Church. The Episcopal Bishop delivered a masterful sermon which was put on the air by our local station. It does one's heart good to see the enthusiasm of these young people.

After the celebration of patriotic week I shall write you again. Thanks for all you have done for us during these years and what do you mean to me today.

Love, Louise Best

*Advocate*, August 1951

# Chapter 24
## Dr. Wil Lou Gray: Evangelist for Education

South Carolina's foremost advocate for adult education and combatting illiteracy was a Methodist-raised and Methodist-educated woman who spent her entire life serving others.

Wil Lou Gray was born in Laurens, South Carolina, in August 1883 and was named for her parents, William L. Gray and Sarah Louise Dial Gray. Her father, a Wofford graduate, was a lawyer and farmer, and her mother had earned her degree from the Methodist-related Spartanburg Female College, two blocks from Wofford. The young Miss Gray had an idyllic childhood in Laurens until the death of her mother shattered that world. She lived with an aunt and uncle until her father remarried, and during that time, she fell behind in her schoolwork. Her stepmother, who had been her first-grade teacher, got her caught up, and she decided that she wanted to be a teacher. Being a Methodist, Columbia College was her obvious choice, and there she thrived.

After graduating from Columbia in 1903, Gray taught in a one-room schoolhouse in Ware Shoals. The next year, she taught in Gray Court, where many of her extended family lived. Students of varying ages required her to teach everything from beginning reading to Latin and algebra. In 1910, she enrolled in graduate school at Columbia University, where she earned a Master of Arts in political science.

Serving in one-room schools brought Gray face to face with adult illiteracy, as many parents could not read messages she sent home or even sign their names. In 1911, she became supervisor of rural schools in Laurens County, and she saw this problem on a countywide basis. While she worked to improve and standardize education throughout the county, she also saw the need for adult education. By

1915, she was organizing night schools for adults. Many of the teachers taught at night for free, but the state's unwillingness to fund the program led her to resign as supervisor of rural work. She had experienced some success, but much more work remained to be done around the state. Her departure actually shamed the state into beginning to fund adult education.

Lured back to the state a year later, she began a thirty-year career as state supervisor of adult schools. She helped create what were sometimes called "lay-by" schools—opportunities for adults to attend school when the crops were "laying-by." Summer schools for adults and young adults became annual events at different colleges in the state, giving hundreds of adults the opportunity to learn.

In 1921, the Upper South Carolina Annual Conference Board of Education appropriated funds to help support an opportunity school at then-Methodist related Lander College. Gray did not limit her focus to Whites but was an early advocate of equal educational opportunities for Black Carolinians. Her biographer noted her belief that African Americans "had proved their patriotism in World War I and should no longer be treated as second-class citizens."

For twenty-five years, Gray worked to educate South Carolinians, but even in 1945, one out of four adult South Carolinians had not completed the fourth grade. At a meeting of Opportunity School alumni at Washington Street Church, a plan was launched to create a permanent Opportunity School. In 1946, at the site of the former Columbia Army Air Base, the South Carolina Opportunity School was established, and she became its first director, a position she held for eleven years.

Gray received numerous awards for her work. In 1947, she became the first woman to receive an honorary doctorate from Wofford, and she also had honorary degrees from Columbia and Winthrop. In 1974, she was inducted into the South Carolina Hall of Fame.

In retirement, she continued to be an advocate for education and equal opportunity until her death, at age one hundred, in 1984.

# Section 3

## Institutions

These columns talk about some of the institutions and organizations of our conference. Some are or were official agencies, while others are voluntary organizations.

# Chapter 25
## The Birth of the *Advocate*, 1837

The *Advocate's* first issue was published in Charleston on June 24, 1837. Much has transpired in the nearly two centuries since the Reverend William Capers, later a bishop, edited the first issue of the paper.

The front page of the first issue contained the following statement explaining the origin and the need for a Methodist publication in the lower South:

> At the late General Conference of the Methodist Episcopal Church, [in 1836] resolutions were passed authorizing the publication of weekly religious papers, on the same footing with the *Christian Advocate and Journal* (New York) and the *Western Christian Advocate* (Cincinnati) in Richmond, Nashville, and Charleston.
>
> The act of the General Conference authorizing these publications was called for by the southern delegates, on the ground of its being necessary to an equal distribution of the benefits of the Church's press to all parts of its communion, and, especially, in view of the peculiar political aspect of the times. Within the range contemplated for the paper at Charleston, leaving equal scope for those at Richmond and Nashville, there are about 50,000 Whites in the membership of the church. Here there are probably 10,000 Methodist families, and a much greater number attached to the Methodists, who have no weekly paper published among them. This, under any circumstances, might be held a sufficient reason for the publication we propose, but considered in connexcion [sic] with the feeling which is known to pervade all classes of men on the subject of our domestic institutions, it not only justifies our undertaking as one that is expedient, but strongly urges it as necessary to the Church.

For those of you who aren't reading between the lines, the "domestic institution" which the editor mentions refers to slavery. By the mid-1830s, White southerners were feeling increasingly defensive about slavery, and the southern delegates to the General Conference (this was eight years before the split) wanted to have publications to defend slavery. Most of the church's publications up to this point were in the North, and therefore they didn't speak with the voice that members of the South Carolina conference wanted to hear. One could actually interpret the founding of *Advocate* publications in Richmond, Charleston, and Nashville as being among the first steps in the schism of American Methodism over slavery.

Lest we think everything about the first issue of the *Advocate* was political, most of the paper contained various stories about the church's missionary work. Reports from Brazil and Argentina took up much of the second page. In a day where most Americans didn't travel very far from home, these must have conjured up exotic images. A report on the eighteenth anniversary meeting of the church's missionary society took several columns. Reports on temperance, on the Bible Society, and even from other denominations took up space on the third page. And in an agricultural society, the paper carried reports of commodity prices in Charleston and the value of various South Carolina bank stocks.

The *Advocate* packed a lot into that first issue. Even at four pages, the paper ran more than 500 column inches—and each column was more than two inches wide, and the print was small.

South Carolina Methodism has evolved quite a bit in the last two centuries, and its voice, the *Advocate*, has evolved along with it.

# Chapter 26
## Spartanburg Female College

Methodists have always been strong supporters of higher education, with more than one hundred schools, colleges and universities having relationships with the denomination today. Over our history, Methodists have had a hand in establishing more than 1,200 educational institutions. Some of these, obviously, no longer exist.

At the same time that they were establishing Wofford for their sons, South Carolina Methodists were concerned about the education of their daughters. During the 1850s, the Annual Conference established colleges for women in Columbia, Spartanburg, and in Anson County, North Carolina, and Lenoir, North Carolina, areas that were then part of the South Carolina Conference.

The Spartanburg Female College opened in August 1855 just a few blocks from the Wofford campus. In fact, College Street got its name because it connected the two Methodist colleges.

Spartanburg's Female College got off to a good start. The trustees reported to the Annual Conference that fifty-three young women were enrolled, and three faculty members were providing instruction in literature, music, languages, geography, astronomy, and physiology. The trustees requested the appointment of the Reverend Charles Taylor, MD, as professor of mathematics and natural sciences, which was approved. He joined J. Wofford Tucker, the president, and instructors Phoebe Paine and St. Pierre Saunier on the faculty. Tucker was a nephew of the Reverend Benjamin Wofford. The college conferred its first degree at Commencement 1857 to Miss C. M. B. Golding, of Laurens, South Carolina.

The college's catalogue described the grounds as "fifteen acres of woodland, on the summit of a hill, overlooking the Town of Spartanburg, and a half-mile, or more, distant from it." The curriculum progressed from the rudiments to "the highest grade of scholarship required at the best female college." Students were taught to think for themselves. The rules were strict; students were not allowed to leave campus unattended, or to visit in the town without the permission of their parents. The only male visitors they were allowed had to be relatives, so "as to preclude the idea of a matrimonial engagement." All letters, notes, books, or papers had to pass to students through the hands of the president.

By 1860, Spartanburg Female College had seen twenty-nine women graduate, and in the fall of that year, about 125 students were enrolled. The trustees expected 150 in the spring term of 1861. The faculty had turned over somewhat in those early years, and the college was on its fourth president by the time of the Civil War. Eight individuals, five of whom were women, were teaching at the college, which was larger than Wofford's faculty at the time. Three of those instructors were in music, and one report noted that the college owned eight pianos. Growth had prompted the trustees to build more buildings, though they were waiting until funds were in hand to complete some of their more ambitious plans.

When the Civil War came, the college remained open. In 1863 and 1864, the college was forced to turn away students for want of room, and revenues were able to meet all the college's expenses. The trustees explained that Spartanburg, which was remote from the war, was thought to be a safe place for a college, and many families who had relocated to the area were sending their daughters there.

The hard times were to come. The college had to suspend operations in 1865, only to reopen in 1866, with considerably reduced enrollment. By 1867, with debts mounting, the conference realized it could no longer support the college and withdrew its patronage. The college was subsequently purchased by Reverend Samuel B. Jones and Samuel Lander.

When the Jones was called to the presidency of Columbia College, the college in Spartanburg closed, and the Reverend R. C. Oliver took charge of the property. Reverend Samuel Lander went on to found the Williamston Female College, which later moved to Greenwood and became Lander College. Oliver operated the Carolina Orphan's Home there for some time, and then the buildings became part of Wofford's preparatory department.

The college's main building saw continued use as part of the Spartan Mill village, as a pellagra hospital, and as a community center for the village, but eventually, even this last trace of the Spartanburg Female College was demolished.

# Chapter 27
## South Carolina's Methodist Women's Colleges

South Carolina's Methodists have taken pride in educating their daughters as well as their sons. At the same time that Wofford College opened for men in 1854, the conference's leaders were planning opportunities to open colleges for women.

The minutes of the 1854 Annual Conference attest to this. "The subject of female education is one highest importance. The movement now on foot, show that although the conference has been late in coming into this field, it means to make up by future activity for past debt."

At least five women's colleges operated at various times within the bounds of the South Carolina Conference. Some no longer exist; one has transformed into a state university, and of course one is still part of the Methodist connection.

The 1854 minutes reported that "the Carolina Female College in Anson County, North Carolina, has been in successful operation for the last four years. As a conference institution it has been exerting a hallowed influence upon the minds and hearts of the young ladies who have been favored with its instructions. … It is commended to the increased attention of the ministers, members, and friends of the church."

The minutes also reflect the conference's direction that colleges for women should be established in Spartanburg and Columbia. In Columbia, land and buildings sufficient to accommodate 200 students were acquired, and the trustees requested the conference appoint a financial agent to raise funds. In Spartanburg, a plot of twenty-three acres had been acquired a half-mile west of the Wofford campus, the trustees had contracted with Clayton and Burgess, the same men who supervised the construction of Wofford's buildings, to build houses for the president and professors. They reported that they expected to be open by the next year. In fact, the Spartanburg college did open in August 1855, with an inaugural address given by William Gilmore Simms.

Spartanburg Female College got off to a good start. However, after the Civil War, the college's debts mounted and it was forced to close. In a way, it was the spiritual ancestor of the Williamston Female College, another college that started with some of the faculty of the Spartanburg Female College. Led by the Reverend Samuel Lander, it opened in Williamston, South Carolina. That college eventually moved to Greenwood, became Lander College, and was a Methodist-related institution until after World War II. Columbia's Female College, of course, did much better, and after a move from downtown, continues to operate.

A final college for women was also in the planning stages in the mid-1850s. Davenport Female College, in Lenoir, North Carolina, opened in 1857. The Reverend Henry Mood was the college's president, and he reported on the curriculum and faculty in the 1858 South Carolina Conference minutes. Lenior and Wadesboro, where the Carolina Female College were located, were both in the South Carolina Conference, at least until 1870.

Once it was organized, the 1866 Conference quickly set about organizing a college, and Claflin University opened in 1869. Interestingly enough, while the historically White conference colleges were single gender, women and men attended Claflin essentially from the beginning. Claflin had a profound influence as it helped form women leaders in the Black church.

# Chapter 28
## The Conference Historical Society: Preserving History Since 1856

The South Carolina Conference has two groups that work to preserve and promote Methodist history in our state. One, the Commission on Archives and History, is elected by the conference to undertake the preservation of the conference's historic records and to support local churches as they preserve their records. Another duty of the commission is to promote the ministry of memory in the Annual Conference and to help plan for historical observances during the year. The *Book of Discipline* also allows the Commission on Archives and History to organize a historical society. But in South Carolina, our Conference Historical Society is much older than the commission.

In November 1856, when the annual conference was meeting in Yorkville, a group of clergy got together to form the Historical Society of the South Carolina Annual Conference. At that meeting, they drafted a constitution and bylaws based on the Baltimore Conference's society. The purpose of the society, according to the constitution, was "to collect and preserve information, in connection with the rise and progress of Methodism within the bounds of the South Carolina Conference and elsewhere; likewise objects of curiosity and interest, in the form of manuscripts, books, pamphlets, medals, portraits, etc., and anything that may shed light upon this interesting subject."

In other words, it was a broad collecting policy that allowed it to accept just about anything that it wanted to take, whether it was about South Carolina specifically or not.

The constitution declared that the property of the society would be deposited at Wofford College. Ever since the society was founded in 1856, Wofford's library has been a repository of the conference's historical records. The society was to meet annually, during the session of the annual conference, to conduct business and to hear a lecture presented on some topic of Methodist history. About seventy members joined as charter members, each agreeing to pay fifty cents as an initiation fee and to donate fifty cents a year to continue their membership.

The Historical Society grew and almost immediately began collecting materials for their library. They asked the sons of two early members of the conference to donate manuscripts and other personal materials of their fathers, and also asked the minister serving in Charleston to acquire some early Charleston church records. Shortly after the conference session, the society's secretary wrote an article for the *Advocate* and the Conference Journal asking support for the new society's work by helping them to collect the conference's historical materials.

"By the collection of books, manuscripts, and etc., the future historian of Southern Methodism will be greatly aided in his labors," he wrote.

The annual address became a feature of the sessions of the Annual Conference, continuing until not very many years ago. Approximately forty of those Historical Society addresses have been digitized and are available today in the digital repository in the Wofford library.

Another point that the secretary made in 1856 was that there was no restriction on membership in the society, "any person favoring our objects and paying the requisite amount may become a member."

In a somewhat different form, the Historical Society still exists today. It is a membership organization that works with the Archives and History Commission to preserve and promote Methodist history in South Carolina and elsewhere. I'm sure the Historical Society would welcome you as a member.

# Chapter 29
## Methodism and Textiles

South Carolina's beginnings were as a rural, agricultural state, and the Methodist Church in South Carolina in those days reflected the state's society. But as time passed, the state saw the growth of more cities and towns, and particularly in the Upcountry, the rise of textiles. And, the church evolved along with society.

Much has been written about the rise of the textile industry in the South, and it was without a doubt one of the most significant changes in our state in the decades after the Civil War and Reconstruction. Many textile workers came to the mills from the mountains and the countryside, and the changes in their lives were dramatic. The Methodist Church felt it needed to be present to minister to the new workers, and in many cases, the conference's Board of Missions worked to support these mill churches financially.

The 1910 Annual Conference, meeting in Charleston, passed two resolutions relating to the growing number of South Carolina Methodists who were working in the textile industry. One related to the support of the work of the church itself, and the conference sought help from mill owners and managers in supporting their work. The other called for stronger laws to prevent child labor, which was commonly practiced in the mills.

### Cotton Mill Commission

WHEREAS, after close and intimate contact with conditions in our mill districts, we conclude that we can not suppose the establishment of proper and permanent machinery on a basis of the revenue derived from the members themselves, because of the frequent changes of these members from mill to mill; and

WHEREAS, the properly manned church is a commercial as well as moral asset of the mills; and

WHEREAS, the lack of funds has prevented in a large measure the securing of efficient ministers for the churches already established; and

WHEREAS, the time is come when the necessity is upon us to place in these fields the best talent the church can secure, with a view to the permanent betterment of the operatives from a spiritual, moral, and intellectual standpoint:

Resolved, That we appeal to the administration of the mills to appropriate to the salaries of the pastors of the different denominations established at these mills a reasonable amount, proportioned according to the amounts paid by the members of the several churches and the Boards of Missions of the denominations interested.

Second, That a commission be appointed from this Conference to confer with a similar commission from other evangelical bodies of the State to bring before the Manufacturers' Association of South Carolina the above outlined proposition at its next session.

## CHILD LABOR

WHEREAS, we have heard with pleasure the address on child labor by Dr. John Porter Hollis; and

WHEREAS, the employment of children of tender age is a serious menace to the future citizenship of South Carolina; and

WHEREAS, the premature toil of children disintegrates families and "depreciates the human stock";

Resolved, That this Conference go on record as heartily favoring the program of the South Carolina Child Labor Committee.

Second, That we memorialize the General Assembly of South Carolina to carefully consider this question, and that it give us such laws as will decrease as far as possible the evils of child labor.

Third, That the Secretary of this Conference be instructed to forward copies of these resolutions to the proper authorities of the South Carolina Legislature.

At its 1911 session, the annual conference endorsed the work of the Reverend David English Camak in founding the Textile Industrial Institute to help educate the state's textile workers. Supported by the Board of Missions, with the encouragement of the Conference Board of Education, TII proved to be a highly successful ministry. Its story is wonderfully told in the book *Common Ties: A*

*History of Textile Industrial Institute, Spartanburg Junior College, and Spartanburg Methodist College*, by Dr. Katherine Davis Cann, who was a professor of history at Spartanburg Methodist College.

As Methodists in South Carolina, we can be proud that we as a church have adapted to changes in our society and have taken stands to correct economic and social problems when we've seen them.

# Chapter 30
## Women's Organizations

Most South Carolina Methodists realize the strong influence and important work of the United Women in Faith in our churches and conference. When did this work begin?

Just after the Civil War, women's efforts moved more into the public sphere, as America entered a period of social reform as well as international missionary work. In the Methodist Episcopal Church, South, the Woman's Foreign Missionary Society was authorized by the General Conference meeting in Atlanta in 1878. This followed years of lobbying the bishops to authorize some type of women's missionary organization. The College of Bishops drafted a constitution, and the wives of the bishops all became vice presidents of the organization. Maria Davies Wightman of South Carolina, the wife of Bishop William M. Wightman, was one of those vice presidents.

In South Carolina, which was one of the fifteen conferences of the Methodist Episcopal Church, South, the Woman's Missionary Society was organized in December 1878, during the meeting of the annual conference in Newberry. A nominating committee, consisting of male members of the annual conference as well as women who would be part of the society recommended a slate of officers.

Maria Wightman was elected president by the forty women in attendance, representing ten charges or stations throughout the conference. The first annual meeting of the Woman's Missionary Society of the South Carolina Conference was held in Trinity Church, Charleston, Wightman's own church, in April 1880. This was reported to be the first time a woman ever presided over a public meeting in South Carolina. Wightman remained the society's president, providing spiritual leadership to their work until her death in 1912.

A second missionary organization, the Parsonage Aid and Home Mission Society (having been organized in the Methodist Church in 1886) was changed to the Woman's Parsonage and Home Mission Society in 1890. In 1898 the organization had the name of the Woman's Home Missionary Society.

In 1910 the General Conference made provisions to unite these two Societies: The Woman's Foreign Missionary Society, thirty-two years old, and The Woman's Home Missionary Society, twenty-five years old. They came together and formed the Woman's Missionary Council of the Methodist Episcopal Church, South. It was optional as to whether the two societies should unite into one conference society, so in South Carolina, the two organizations did not unite until the Conference split into two Annual Conferences in 1914.

The women of the South Carolina Conference met January 22, 1915, in Florence and organized. The women of the Upper South Carolina Conference also met the same year and organized as the Woman's Missionary Society of the Upper South Carolina Conference, thus bringing home and foreign mission work into a single organization for each conference.

In 1940, after Methodist reunification, the society had another name change. Both upper and South Carolina conference societies became the Woman's Society of Christian Service of their respective conference. In October 1948, when the two conferences merged back together, the Woman's Societies of Christian Service also merged. And, after the creation of The United Methodist Church in 1968, the United Methodist Women's organization was born.

For more information about the history of our conference's women's organizations, you can read *Daring Hearts and Spirits Free: South Carolina Women in the United Methodist Tradition*, edited by Harriet Anderson Mays and Harry Roy Mays.

# Section 4

## History

These columns talk about the overall history of our annual conference and how it has evolved over the years. They also address the history of The United Methodist Church, with some columns about milestones in the history of the denomination. A few address notable figures in the history of world Methodism.

# Chapter 31
## The Sancho Letter

*Author's note: One of the hidden treasures in the archives is a letter written by an enslaved Carolinian named Sancho Cooper, who was converted to Methodism by Bishop Francis Asbury sometime around 1800. This letter is part of the H. A. C. Walker Papers in the Wofford Archives. It's a fascinating, painful, and moving story of suffering and forgiveness. As I've noted earlier, part of the mission of the archives is to preserve our past and to connect us to our past. As difficult as it is, we as South Carolinians and Methodists should always remember that not everything in our history is happy. Still, stories such as this can teach us about strength in times of suffering as well as grace.*

I Sancho was born in the city of Cowbo, Africa, and I was raised by my parents in the fear of God, the same God that I now adore. My father worshipped him before me. The name of God was Ala and the name of Christ was Mamudda, in my native language. At about twelve years of age my father sent me to England for the purpose of giving me schooling under the care of Mr. Price, but alas for us we were overtooken by robbers, captured, and carried to Jamaica. We remained there one year. The captain of our vessel was hung. After remaining there one year, I was brought over to South Carolina and fell into the hands of a Mr. Canada, a Roman Catholic. About fifteen or twenty years after I lived in South Carolina, I embraced religion. I got powerfully awakened under the labors of Bishop Ashbury [sic] in Charleston and never gave up the struggle until I was happily converted to God, through the mercy of our Lord and Saviour Jesus Christ.

Now my troubles began. My master Canada hated from his soul the Methodists and I was most cruelly treated on that account. Only God who knows all this knows the suffering that I endured with that man for seven years, oft times being so washed in my blood and made to pull him in his sulky instead of a horse every evening with a double-barreled gun in his hand to shoot me down if I should run. Yet amidst all of this severe treatment I rejoyce [sic] in it and my soul was happy. At the end of seven years he died. He sent for me to pray for him during his illness.

After his death a captain Randall bought me. He was an Episcopalian and I told him I was a Methodist. He also hated the Methodists. I held prayer meetings on his plantation. He heard of it and called for me and told me he heard that I held meetings on his plantation and told me if I do the like again, he would slay me down with his sword. But blest be the name of God, I found that threats of swords, burned fires, and lions are no obstacles in the way of souls on fire with heavenly love. I still held prayers on his plantation. He came and found me praying, and he had a sword and pistole [sic] in his hand and made a threat at me with his sword. But the sword broke in his hand. But he took me and had me tied to an apple tree and one hundred and fifty lashes put upon me and told me to call upon Christ to take it off. And also said that __ Christ himself. He then put me in the barn in storks and a chain fixed upon my neck. I told him he could rile my body but could not hurt the soul. I laid in that situation all night covered with blood in storks neck with chain fixed upon it, and O Paul, I know the reason why you and your comrade sang praises to God in midnight when you was in prison as one might suffering for Jesus is a happy time for the sufferer. When I came out next morning he was ashamed and some of the people fainted at the sight of me. But I felt happy and bold and strong. I told him that he hated God and he hated the word of God and I heard in my own country that the people in this country was a barbarous peoples. He drove me off his plantation.

He sold me to Dr. Cooper so that he should broke me of my religion. I had many conversations with him about religion. He said he liked the Methodists and said that his father had died a Methodist and that he himself was a Methodist. He however tried my faith and also my honesty and found me an honest and upright and faithful servant. For the religion of our blessed Lord and Saviour acts these traits to a man's character and makes him shine brighter and brighter unto the perfect day. After trying me in various ways and still finding the same consistent servant, he allowed me great privileges. He allowed me to sing praises and pray and hold meetings in and through his yard. He also made me steward over his yard. I was made the principal purchaser of the necessarys of his yard not regaining any in numeratory with me for moneys spent. But under this great exhortation I did not get proud but still kept my heart under subjection giving honor and praise unto his holy name that he calls me a lonely and poor African in a strange land to gain the confidence of my earthly master in surpassing my heart with that religion that makest wise the simple and is a friend to the friendly and the poor.

I love the Methodist church. I love her ways. I have been fighting under her banners for fifty-three or -four years as far as I can recollect, and by the grace of God I intend to stand with her until life's latest hour. Any prayers shall be offered in her behalf while I have breath to breathe. When I consider the great kindness and considerations she sent, the sacrifices she makes of health and property in sending her ministers through thick and thin, through hot and cold, through the ditches of the rice fields and cotton patches, that the poor untutored African may have the gospel preached unto him and his soul pointed to Christ. O thou church of my God, go on in thy labor of love and many stars shall be added to thy crown.

I have heard of the shouts of the dying African as he blessed God that he ever raised up such a company of men as to care thus for their souls. I feel my time now drawing to an end and I bless God that I feel able to say with an apostle for I am now ready to be offered, and the time of my departure is at hand. I have fought a good fight, I have finished my course, I have kept the faith, henceforth there is laid up for me a crown of righteousness which the Lord, the righteous judge shall give me at that day and not to me only but to all them also that have love his appearing.

This may be the last conference year that I ever expect to spend this side of eternity. It is my prayer day and night that God would pour out his spirit and that he would revive his works abundantly and that it may extend to all people both White and Black.

# Chapter 32
## Slavery and the First Great Methodist Schism, 1844

A great controversy divided Methodists in the nineteenth century, one where members had deeply held beliefs about an issue. These views hardened over several decades, and when they realized that their views had become irreconcilable, at a General Conference in 1844, they agreed to an amicable separation. In this case, the issue was that of slavery.

From our earliest days, Methodists talked about slavery. John Wesley was a strong opponent, and as early as 1743, he had prohibited his followers from buying or selling the bodies and souls of men, women, and children with an intention to enslave them. The 1784 Christmas Conference listed slaveholding as an offense for which one could be expelled.

However, in a sign that the church would face conflicts over this issue, the 1785 General Conference suspended that provision. Methodists in South Carolina and other southern states evangelized among the slaves, eventually appointing ministers to serve on the plantations. By 1795, according to conference historian Dr. A.V. Huff, several South Carolina and Virginia ministers signed covenants not to hold slaves in any state where the law would allow them to manumit them, on pain of forfeiting their honor and their place in the itinerancy. If the state would not allow manumission, they agreed to pay the slave for his or her labor.

But Methodists struggled with how to square their denomination's opposition to the peculiar institution in a country where slavery was legal, and in some parts of the country, widely supported. And after 1792, slavery began to grow more popular in the Deep South. The invention of the cotton gin suddenly made growing upland cotton more profitable, and it made more South Carolina farmers want more slaves to grow more cotton. The backcountry farmers the church wanted to attract suddenly became more supportive of the institution of slavery. As the church was hoping for emancipation, society was growing more committed to slavery.

When copies of the General Conference's 1800 "Affectionate Address on the Evils of Slavery" arrived in Charleston, a storm erupted. John Harper, who gave out copies, suddenly found himself targeted for spreading abolitionist propaganda. He escaped, but his colleague George Dougherty was nearly drowned under a pump. Bishop Francis Asbury himself made a personal compromise. If it came to evangelizing the South or upholding the Wesleyan antislavery position, antislavery had to go. In 1804, he would not allow General Conference to take a stronger antislavery position. He allowed the printing of two *Disciplines* that year—one with the portion on slavery omitted for South Carolina

Several General Conferences struggled with the issue, first pressing clergy to emancipate their slaves, then suspending those rules in states where the laws did not permit manumission. By 1808, General Conference threw up its hands, finding the subject unmanageable, and gave each annual conference the right to enact its own rules relative to slaveholding.

The denomination remained divided on slavery, as some northern Methodists became more convinced of slavery's evil and some southern Methodists more convinced that it was a positive good. Other southerners felt that any denunciation of slaveholding by Methodists would damage the church in the South. They were caught, in effect, between church rules and state laws.

The spark that caused the division came when Bishop James O. Andrew, a Georgian and a former member of the South Carolina Conference, become a slaveholder through inheritance. Many northern Methodists were appalled that a bishop who might have authority over them could also own slaves. When General Conference convened in New York City on May 1, 1844, this would be the main topic for debate. The six-week session would be the longest General Conference in Methodist history.

Bishop Andrew first resolved to resign from the episcopacy, but some southern delegates persuaded him that his resignation would "inflict an incurable wound on the whole South and inevitably lead to division in the church." The General Conference asked Andrew for details about his situation. Bishop Andrew explained that first, he had inherited an enslaved woman from a woman in Augusta, Georgia, who had asked him to care for her until she turned nineteen, and then emancipate her and send her to Liberia, and if she declined to go, then he should make her "as free as the laws of Georgia would permit." The young woman refused to go, so she lived in her own home on his lot and was free to go to the North if she wished, but until then she was legally his slave. He also inherited an enslaved man through his first wife who would also be free to leave whenever he was able to provide for himself. His second wife had also brought enslaved persons to their marriage, but he disclaimed ownership of them. "I have neither bought nor sold a slave," he told the General Conference, "and in the state where I am legally a slaveholder, emancipation is impracticable."

A group of northern delegates proposed a resolution that the bishop was "hereby affectionately asked to resign." Some delegates took the position that the bishops were officers elected by the General Conference and could be asked to resign or deposed by majority vote. Others took the view that it was a constitutional office and bishops could be removed only by judicial process. A substitute resolution by one of the bishop's friends, an Ohioan, asked the bishop to desist from exercising his office as long as he was a slaveholder. After a twelve-day debate, other efforts at compromise—including one that would have allowed Andrew to serve wherever he would be welcomed—failed when it became apparent that the New England conferences would secede if it passed.

One of the prominent speakers in the debate was William Capers, who was the leader of South Carolina's delegation and a future bishop. Whatever the resolution, some segment of the church was going to leave.

The motion asking Andrew to desist from serving as a bishop passed, 111-69. General Conference then worked through the beginnings of a plan of separation, appointing a committee of nine members to draft a plan. Some disagreements continued for a few years over church assets, such as the publishing house. Southern Annual Conferences sent delegates to a convention in Louisville in May 1845, where they formed the Methodist Episcopal Church, South.

For the next ninety-four years, the two strands of the Methodist Episcopal Church operated separately. Their separation was one of the turning points on the road to the American Civil War, for the Methodist Church was one of several national churches and institutions that broke apart because it could not withstand the growing tensions surrounding the divisive issue of slavery.

# Chapter 33
## The Beginning of the 1866 Conference

At 9:00 on the morning of April 2, 1866, Bishop Osman C. Baker convened a meeting of the Methodist missionaries who were serving members of the Methodist Episcopal Church, South, in South Carolina. These ministers were working among the state's recently emancipated people of color, and the bishop had convened them to create a new annual conference.

After a time of worship, Bishop Baker read a resolution of the previous General Conference that permitted the creation of missionary annual conferences when deemed necessary. Fourteen clergy members became the first members of the new South Carolina Missionary Conference of the Methodist Episcopal Church, South. The new conference covered South Carolina, Eastern Georgia, and Florida, and consisted of some twelve pastoral charges (seven in South Carolina, five in Florida).

The events of the first week of April 1866 did not mark the beginning of Black Methodism in South Carolina. Though enslaved, many thousands of men and women had worshipped in South Carolina Methodist churches for eighty years or more. Before the Civil War, White clergy as well as African-American lay preachers and class leaders had brought the word, and often the balconies, or galleries, of Charleston's churches were filled with Black Methodists. The Civil War brought a new chapter in that history, especially in the areas around Beaufort after the Union Army captured the Sea Islands in November 1861. There the first Northern Methodist missionaries came to serve the freedmen. In 1865, with the war over, both White and Black Methodists had to adjust to new circumstances.

White Methodists hoped and planned to resume the pre-war custom of White control of the church, with White parishioners sitting on the main floor of the sanctuaries and African-American Methodists sitting in the galleries. Property disputes abounded in Charleston, and attempts at compromise had faltered when an announcement of a settlement was to happen at Trinity Methodist. There, before any decision had been rendered as to how the freedmen would be treated, the Reverend T. Willard Lewis rose and shouted, "Brothers and sisters, there will be no galleries in heaven, those who care to go with a church that makes no distinctions as to race or color, follow me to the Normal School at the corner of Beaufain and St. Philip Streets." And from that point, South Carolina's Black Methodists declared their independence.

The Reverends V. H. Bulkly and James R. Rosemond were the first Black clergy to lead congregations in the new conference. Reverend Bulkly served largely around Charleston, and Reverend Rosemond is remembered for founding numerous churches in York, Spartanburg, Greenville, Anderson, and Oconee counties.

The *Advocate* of the 1860s did not report on these happenings—the southern church's General Conference was meeting in New Orleans in April 1866, and the pages of the *Advocate* were full of the daily proceedings. But the paper did publish several opinion pieces from around the South that were critical of the northern missionaries who were working in the South. Many of the articles expressed bitterness over the way they felt they had been mistreated by the national government, and even somehow that the northern branch of Methodism had misrepresented their positions.

The shock and dismay around the end of an era would linger for generations among White Carolinians, but the creation of the 1866 Conference marked a new day dawning for Black Carolinians. They moved forward with a new hope and a sense of purpose and set about creating new institutions, such as the church, where they could lead a free people and create a new community.

Much of this information comes from the Reverend Warren M. Jenkins' book *Steps Along the Way: The Origins and Development of the South Carolina Conference of the Central Jurisdiction*, published in 1967.

# Chapter 34
## Methodism and Race in South Carolina

Part of the role of archives and history is to note significant anniversary events in our shared life and lift them up so we can remember them and reflect on what they might still mean for us today.

Methodists, like any other group with a long history in South Carolina, have had to face questions of race and relations between Black and White church members throughout our history. A number of anniversaries give us ample opportunities to talk more about these questions as well as the ways we have evolved into the conference we are today.

The year 2016 marked the 150th anniversary of the founding of what has been historically known as the South Carolina Conference (1866), the conference established by the northern branch of Methodism to minister to African Americans in the Palmetto State. The General Conference in 1864 had authorized creating missionary conferences in the former Confederacy, and it was under this authority that a missionary Annual Conference convened on April 2, 1866, under the leadership of Bishop Osman C. Baker. Its first members of the conference were the northern missionary clergy, but on its first day, that conference admitted five Black members. The new missionary conference initially consisted of twelve pastoral charges, seven in South Carolina and five in northern Florida. From that beginning came a century's work in church building, education, and outreach in South Carolina.

The need for ministerial education was immediately recognized, and the Baker Theological Institute was organized in Charleston. Dozens of men attended the institute for further ministerial study, and over the next few years, they were ordained into the ministry and joined the South Carolina Conference. Three years later, the conference established a university, the funds for which came from Lee Claflin and his son, Massachusetts Governor William Claflin. In 1870, the South Carolina Conference met at Claflin University. Claflin and the conference became almost one and the same over the next decades. The state's African-American Methodist clergy were educated there, as were teachers for the state's Black schools. Those individuals spread out throughout the state, founding churches in communities far and wide.

From 1866 to 1939, the two South Carolina conferences, with their founding dates of 1785 and 1866, were technically part of two different denominations. They knew each other existed and even shared a common tradition, but they had separate ecclesiastical structures, different bishops, and different Books of Discipline. Much of that changed in 1939, when the three branches of American Methodism, after being divided for close to a century, and after two decades of negotiations, formally reunified into the Methodist Church.

However, merger did not happen at the conference level, and as a compromise, the jurisdictions were created. African-American Methodists were placed into a racially segregated Central Jurisdiction, and as such, South Carolina's White and African American Methodists remained in separate annual conferences with separate bishops.

Movements in the Methodist Church throughout the 1950s and 1960s sought to eliminate the Central Jurisdiction, and much of the turmoil in South Carolina Methodism fifty years ago revolved around how to resolve these issues.

# Chapter 35
## Dividing the Conference, 1914

When South Carolina's Methodists gathered for Annual Conference in 1914, one of the hot topics for discussion was how to divide the conference into two new annual conferences.

At the 1913 session, the South Carolina Conference (1785) requested to be split into two smaller conferences. The 1914 General Conference of the Methodist Episcopal Church, South, approved the division, but left it to the annual conference to draw the dividing line and handle the division of conference property. Within the South Carolina Conference, some members who opposed the split questioned the legality of General Conference voting to divide the conference without drawing the new boundaries itself. Their articles in the *Advocate* suggest they did not believe division was a done deal; they believed the vote in 1913 to divide in two was so close that the next conference could either revisit it or rescind it. They tried to derail the plan, appealing on several points of law to the presiding bishop, Collins Denny.

Bishop Denny, however, overruled these points, saying he lacked the authority to rule an act of the General Conference unconstitutional by himself. That authority, he said, rested with the entire College of Bishops alone.

With Denny refusing to overturn the action of General Conference, the annual conference proceeded to debate how to draw the new boundary. It should come as no surprise to anyone who has ever attended annual conference that the debates on how to divide the conference were hot, and the conference soon got itself tied in parliamentary knots. Several ministers proposed different plans of division.

The principal plan was devised by the Reverend E. O. Watson, who was the secretary of the annual conference. Watson's proposed line essentially ran along the Sandhills, starting along the Chesterfield-Lancaster county border, running along the Lancaster-Kershaw and Fairfield-Kershaw county lines, crossing Richland County, then running between Lexington and Calhoun, and then along the southern border of Aiken County. He said he opposed dividing the state into an eastern and western or a northern and southern conference.

What reasons did Watson give for supporting the division of the conference? He believed two cabinets could make better matches between clergy and churches if they only had to make 125 or 130 appointments rather than twice that number. Having an upper and a lower conference, he believed, would let each focus on the particular mission-related needs of each part of the state. The upper conference would be better able to work on the "mill problem" that South Carolina progressives were talking about, and the lower conference had more rural issues to consider. Finally, dividing the conference would allow clergy to serve more consistently in a part of the state where they were better suited to serve or more interested in serving

Watson found some critics, including the editorial writer of the *Advocate*, who argued that the upper conference would have about as many rural charges as the lower. One writer said he believed the upper conference would not be able to afford its financial obligations, particularly to mill churches that were operating with conference support. Some members of the conference evidently believed that if they could defeat all of the proposed boundaries, then the vote of General Conference to divide the conference would be rendered moot.

This was not to be the case. First, a motion to postpone the division and request General Conference to rescind its approval failed by a vote of 130-122. After several days of debate, and after defeating a few other plans for division, a line very similar to the one proposed by the conference secretary was approved.

When the appointments were read, about half of the clergy found themselves in the new Upper South Carolina Conference, which would go on to hold its first session in 1915 at Bethel, Spartanburg.

The two conferences would remain separate through 1947 and would reunite in 1948 after a new General Conference remerged them.

# Chapter 36
## Methodist Reunification, 1939

I've written about the division of the Methodist Episcopal Church into northern and southern branches in 1845, largely over the issue of slavery. Since we're members today of The United Methodist Church, we know that at some point, we got back together. When did that happen?

The northern and southern branches of the Methodist Episcopal Church, along with the Methodist Protestant Church, joined to create The Methodist Church in 1939 at a uniting General Conference in Kansas City, Missouri. Reunification came about after two generations of movement in that direction, and several South Carolina Methodists were instrumental in that movement. Dr. Henry Nelson Snyder, Wofford's president from 1902 to 1942, was a member of the reunification commission that first convened in 1916.

The division in the church had occurred in the generation before the American Civil War, and in the generation following the war, Methodists on both sides of the Mason-Dixon Line began reaching out to each other. They recognized that they shared a common tradition and knew that good relations between the two denominations would have to grow before any further steps toward cooperation might ever happen.

Beginning in the late 1870s, some sixty years before formal union, the two churches were sending fraternal delegates to each other's General Conference. By the 1890s, the two churches were willing to create a joint Commission on Federation, though they were still far from any plan of union. The joint commission looked for and found areas where the two denominations could work together, such as on publishing and on foreign missions. Tensions still existed, however, as both churches were seeking new members in the western states.

At a major conference in 1910, delegates from all three denominations agreed to study a union of the churches, not simply a federation.

The thorny American problem of race relations, however, reared its head, and a proposal coming out of this group would have placed all of the African-American members of the new denomination into a separate "Quadrennial Conference" as the regional bodies we now know as jurisdictions were tentatively named.

By 1916, the Commission on Federation became a joint commission on unification, with a goal of creating a new denomination. It met some six times in the next three years to perfect a plan of union. Still, the role of African-American members was of primary concern to the southern delegates. And the churches early on decided on the need for an independent judicial council, for whereas the southern church relied on the College of Bishops as the final arbiter of the church constitution, the northern church relied on the General Conference to hold that role.

By 1920, a new constitution had been proposed, both general conferences had considered it, and in 1924, both general conferences approved it and submitted it to the annual conferences for approval. It required a three-fourths vote of all of the southern annual conferences to go into effect.

However, many southern Methodists objected to unification in the mid-1920s, fearing integration, social liberalism, loss of control of the church, loss of identity, and even that northern ministers would come south and take all the better appointments. When the votes of the annual conferences were tallied, a majority had approved, but nowhere near the three-fourths majority required.

This proved to be only a temporary setback. Several powerful bishops had opposed the plan, as had many members of the laity. But Methodist young people were strong supporters of church union. By 1935, all three denominations were using the same hymnal, one that the three denominations had worked to develop. The churches agreed on the jurisdictional system as the basis for uniting the church, and they also agreed on the need for equal representation of the laity and clergy in each annual conference.

In 1936, the General Conferences of the Methodist Protestant and Methodist Episcopal churches approved the plan of union, and their annual conferences moved quickly to ratify. In the south, the annual conferences acted first, and about eighty-six percent of the members of the conferences approved. Approval of the southern General Conference was almost a foregone conclusion in 1938. The Uniting General Conference convened on April 26, 1939.

Reunification, however, brought about some unwelcome compromises. Black

Methodists were placed into a segregated Central Jurisdiction, and as such, the South Carolina Conference (1866) became the South Carolina Conference, Central Jurisdiction, with bishops elected by that jurisdiction. The jurisdictional conference itself was the compromise that brought about reunification, as many southerners wanted bishops to be selected within each region.

The Central Jurisdiction existed until it was abolished in 1968, which was the same time that The United Methodist Church was created.

# Chapter 37
## The First Southeastern Jurisdictional Conference

Every four years, Methodists all over the United States gather for jurisdictional conferences, where in each of the five jurisdictions, they carry out the church's business for that area of the country. Perhaps most visibly, they elect bishops to lead the annual conferences within each jurisdiction. They also hear reports, adopt budgets, and celebrate ministry in the parts of the connection.

How did we get jurisdictions? They were created as a byproduct of the reunification of the three principal branches of Methodism in 1939. In that year, the Methodist Episcopal, Methodist Episcopal South, and Methodist Protestant churches combined to form The Methodist Church, healing a schism dating to the 1840s.

Reunification was not a smooth path, and earlier attempts had been voted down by southern conferences fearful of losing their voice in the larger church. The question of race loomed large over reunification, as in most southern and many border states, separate annual conferences had been organized for Black Methodists. These conferences had been organized under the authority of the northern branch of the church, but reunification would erase that distinction. Most White southerners were not interested in integrating the denomination, and beyond that, they did not want a unified church's General Conference electing bishops for the southern conferences. So, the jurisdictional system was devised to work around these concerns, with five regional bodies and one, the Central Jurisdiction, designed to gather all the African-American membership conferences.

The first session of the Southeastern Jurisdictional Conference met in Asheville, North Carolina, from May 23-27, 1940. It was the first of the six jurisdictional conferences to convene, and the conference's sessions were held in

Asheville's municipal auditorium. The first General Conference following reunification had been held only a month earlier, so the delegates might have been a little tired of conferencing when they arrived.

Ten delegates represented the South Carolina Conference, and fourteen represented the Upper South Carolina Conference. The lead lay delegate from the Upper South Carolina Conference was Wofford's President Henry Nelson Snyder, who was no newcomer to conferencing. He had been a member of every General Conference but one since 1906 and had also served on the Joint Hymnal Commission and on the Reunification Commission.

The first SEJ Conference consisted of eighteen annual conferences—including the Cuba Annual Conference—in the states from Mississippi to Kentucky to Virginia. By membership, the SEJ was the largest of the jurisdictions. Eight effective and four retired bishops were part of the jurisdiction, and the senior effective bishop, Urban V. W. Darlington, was tasked with calling the first conference to order.

With eight bishops in the jurisdiction, the conference actually did not have to elect any new bishops, but it did have to make episcopal area assignments for the quadrennium. South Carolina received a new bishop to preside over the South Carolina and Upper South Carolina conferences.

William T. Watkins—who had been elected at the last Methodist Episcopal, South, General Conference in 1938, had previously served in the St. Louis area and the Memphis area, and at forty-four was the youngest bishop in the jurisdiction—became the first bishop assigned to South Carolina by the Southeastern Jurisdiction.

# Chapter 38

## The 1964 General Conference

News of the 1964 General Conference dominated the pages of the *Advocate* in May 1964.

The 1964 General Conference met in Pittsburgh, with some 850 delegates in attendance. South Carolina was represented by two delegations, as the Black and White conferences had not yet merged. Fourteen delegates represented the 1785 conference and four represented the 1866 Conference. Bishop Paul Hardin Jr. was there, as were many spouses of the almost all-male delegations. (The 1866 Conference had elected one woman, Mrs. Beulah Baxley, as a lay delegate.)

The *Advocate* noted several other visitors from South Carolina to the conference. The Columbia College Choir, on its spring tour in April and May 1964, sang at one of the morning devotional services as well as at an afternoon preaching service. (The choir sang at several Methodist churches on the way to and back from Pittsburgh.)

Issues of unity and division faced the General Conference. The system of segregated annual and jurisdictional conferences was receiving great scrutiny and criticism. Two South Carolina churches submitted petitions to retain the system that had been created in 1939. However, the Methodist Church was in the final stages of negotiating a merger with the Evangelical United Brethren Church, and that church would not join a church that still practiced segregation.

After a lengthy debate, the General Conference took the first steps toward dismantling the Central Jurisdiction. It made the moves voluntary, but if all the annual conferences in the Central Jurisdiction had not moved into the geographic jurisdictions by 1968, it would take steps to make it mandatory. The delegates also passed a strong statement against segregation, noting "The Methodist Church is part of the church universal, therefore, all persons without regard to race, color, national origin, or economic condition, shall be eligible to attend its worship services, participate in its programs, and be admitted to membership anywhere in this connection."

Changes in the world also were apparent in Pittsburgh. Bishop Hardin wrote in his column about the Council of Bishops meetings where the central conference and autonomous church bishops reported on the unrest in other parts of the world. The 1960s were seeing many countries in developing parts of the world achieve independence.

At the same time, the Methodist Church was beginning to reckon with what it meant to be a worldwide church. At the meeting, the General Conference also approved a new hymnal and a new *Book of Worship* and increased its world service funding.

A few amusing events made the news. The civic auditorium had a roof that could be rolled open. At one of the evening worship services, the organizers arranged for the roof of the auditorium to roll open during the singing of "How Great Thou Art," which brought a great reaction from the audience. However, this caused something of an updraft, making the curtains whip on the stage and the cross begin to sway.

Another note that no doubt caused amusement was that the week after the General Conference, a circus was scheduled to move into the civic arena. The jokes probably wrote themselves.

# Chapter 39

## Selma 1965, as One Editor Saw It

In March 1965, a group of civil rights protesters met Alabama state and local lawmen on the Edmund Pettus Bridge in Selma, Alabama. The protesters were beginning a march from Selma to Montgomery to protest the lack of voting rights for African Americans in Alabama and much of the rest of the South. A recent movie, Selma, has brought renewed attention to the events surrounding what came to be called "Bloody Sunday," and no doubt there will be other remembrances of those events in coming weeks.

*Advocate* editor the Reverend McKay Brabham wrote a long essay in the March 18, 1965 *Advocate* about the events of March 7 and the following days. Here are some excerpts, which appear to have been influenced by his attendance at a meeting of religious leaders in Washington:

> No mistake should be made at this point: The Commission on Religion and Race of the National Council of Churches of Christ in the U.S.A. is every bit the potent pressure group its friends or critics claim that it is. Certainly its impact upon the President of the United States must be recognized as formidable if the Commission is given its share of credit, as it should be, for his presence before the Congress last Monday evening [where President Johnson called for passage of a voting rights act]. …
>
> It was clear from the meeting last Friday … that the skilled and dedicated leadership of the commission is committed without question to absolute equality before the law for all people. It is also evident that the Commission's leaders are equally willing to take the word of Dr. Martin

Luther King and those associated with him as to legal or other strategic means for achieving it. The Commission operates under a mandate from the General Board given in 1963, "to do everything possible by Christian, non-violent means to work for the achievement of racial justice in the nation."

Reverend Brabham had, by the mid-1960s, earned a reputation as a believer in social justice. He likely found himself in a position like other White southern moderates and liberals in that he supported the aims of the civil rights movement, but not always the tactics.

And, no doubt at this meeting in Washington, he felt somewhat uncomfortable because he was a White southern clergyman, for his editorial noted the following:

> To many of them [at this meeting], the White Southerner has committed the completely unforgivable sin of being White and living in the South. They are therefore to be written off as of no importance to God or man.
>
> Those Christians who seek to maintain a concern for all of God's children—of all colors—must reckon with this fact in their efforts to exercise the force of reconciliation in our time. Without an understanding of its emotional impact and its power over men's minds and wills, they stand to be ready victims of traps such as enmeshed the police of Alabama at Selma when their unleashed brutality provided the springboard for Selma's dive into world history.
>
> Selma did provide an occasion for real heroism and spiritual power, according to what we could learn from those who had gone there on Monday and Tuesday, and who shared the fears of the Negro community. The listener did not have to agree with the tactics [of the march] to appreciate the response of faith on the part of those who felt called to witness in Selma.

# Chapter 40

## The United Methodist Church Turns Fifty

*Author's note: This was jointly authored with Allison Trussell.*

On April 23, 1968, Bishop Reuben H. Mueller of the Evangelical United Brethren Church and Bishop Lloyd C. Wicke of the Methodist Church joined hands over symbolic items and said, "Lord of the Church, we are united in thee, in thy Church, and now in The United Methodist Church."

With that pronouncement, The United Methodist Church became the second largest denomination with nearly twelve million members worldwide.

The Evangelical United Brethren Church, or EUB, had been formed in 1944 by the merger of the Evangelical Church and the Church of the United Brethren in Christ. The EUB Church traced its origins to work among German-speaking settlers at the same time as the Methodists were working among the English-speaking settlers. In 1968, there were about 750,000 members of the EUB Church, though there were no congregations in South Carolina.

Bob Lear, head of the Church Bureau of Methodist Information, wrote in the May 2, 1968, Advocate that "the ceremonies in Dallas were the conclusion of conversation that began as early as 1803 and mark the first union among the denominations participating in the Consultation on Church Union." The Uniting Conference followed the approval of Plan of Union by the General Conferences of both churches in 1966. That plan was perfected at the 1968 conference by a joint committee.

South Carolina's two annual conferences were represented by twenty delegates: the Reverend Adlai C. Holler, Rev. C. LeGrande Moody Jr., Rev. Francis

T. Cunningham, Rev. R. Wright Spears, Rev. W. Wallace Fridy, Rev. Samuel R. Glenn, Rev. Victor Hickman, Rev. Eben Taylor, W. J. Ready, J. Emmett Jerome, Harry Kent, Spencer M. Rice, J. Carlisle Holler, Dr. Charles F. Marsh, Roy C. Moore and W. L. Brannon represented the White conference, and Rev. Warren M. Jenkins, Rev. C. Jasper Smith, R. J. Palmer, and Richard E. Fields represented the Black conference.

The May 9 *Advocate* invited delegates to offer their impressions on the two-week conference.

ReverendHoller, the previous editor of the *Advocate*, wrote, "We are off to a good start but it will require heart searching and patience as we adjust … and strive to find the guidance for the new structure. … Our emphasis will continue to be on developing people to that they may become good witnesses for Christ."

Dr. Spears and others emphasized the worldwide role of the new church: "Methodism has assumed a wide role, by uniting with the Evangelical United Brethren, in ecumenicity. What an opportunity in the total world Christian movement!"

The 1968 conference also ended segregation within the church. Although the northern and southern branches of Methodism had reunited in 1939 to form The Methodist Church, African-American congregations remained segregated in a separate Central Jurisdiction. The uniting of the two denominations saw the abolition of the Central Jurisdiction. From 1968 to 1972, the two South Carolina conferences, Black and White, operated side by side, with Bishop Paul Hardin Jr. serving as bishop of both conferences.

South Carolina completed the merger of its Black and White conferences in June 1972.

The Reverend Cunningham noted the challenges facing the new church: "Because we live in a world of ferment, the Church is in ferment. We are a world Church. Let us accept the inevitability of controversy, love each other, seek the facts, and express our convictions as Christian brothers across all dividing lines created by man."

Although the new church was created in 1968, delegates realized all the work of restricting board and agencies could not be completed, and a special session of General Conference was held in 1970 in St. Louis.

# Chapter 41

## Prelude to Merger: Creating a Single South Carolina Annual Conference

With the words "Lord of the Church, we are united in Thee, in Thy Church and now in The United Methodist Church," proclaimed in Dallas, Texas, on April 23, 1968, our denomination came into being. South Carolina Methodists became United Methodists. While that was the only immediate change that the new church brought to the Palmetto State, the events of April 1968 laid the groundwork for major changes in South Carolina Methodism.

As part of the agreement to unite, the Methodists and Evangelical United Brethren churches agreed to eliminate the structures that segregated Black and White Methodists into separate conferences. The move to abolish the Central Jurisdiction had been in the works almost since it was created, and the EUBs were not willing to join until it was gone. The abolition of the Central Jurisdiction satisfied the EUB demands, but it came with no promise from the General Conference of equitable treatment in representation, service on boards or commissions, or anything else. Some Central Jurisdiction leaders voiced concerns about losing leadership opportunities that the Central Jurisdiction afforded them.

With the abolition of the Central Jurisdiction, the annual conferences in the South had to begin to work on plans to merge.

South Carolina's 1866 and 1785 conferences had already appointed a joint committee on merger. The process was slow to unfold. The *Advocate* did begin to report more on the activities in the 1866 Conference, no doubt an intentional decision that the Reverend McKay Brabham, the editor, made. After 1968,

Resident Bishop Paul Hardin Jr. became the bishop of both the 1866 and 1785 conferences, and he talked about both conferences in his columns.

In May 1970, just before the 1866 Conference convened at Claflin University, the first draft of the merger document was presented. The report noted the desire for the merger to be just that: a genuine merger, and not an absorption of the smaller (40,000 member) 1866 Conference into the larger (195,000 member) 1785 Conference. The plan also set a formula for board and commission membership, the number of districts, and blocked any changes in the conference standing rules that would undermine the merger agreement for twelve years.

Letters to the *Advocate* from White Methodists throughout the fall of 1970 generally opposed merger. When the initial plan of merger was presented to the 1866 Conference in May 1971, it passed, but when the 1785 Conference met two weeks later, they voted to reject the plan. A committee from the 1785 conference met to propose changes, and a special session of the 1785 conference was called for September to evaluate options.

In September 1971, the 1785 Conference approved a plan of merger with a set of changes. Evidently they did not consult with the 1866 Conference, for a few weeks later, a special session of the 1866 conference rejected the new plan. They appointed their own committee to negotiate.

In January 1972, a joint session of both annual conferences considered and agreed on a merger plan. Out of that process, messy as it was, came a plan that was acceptable to both conferences, and with the details ironed out, merger took place in June 1972.

# Chapter 42

## Becoming One Annual Conference

The year 2022 marked the fiftieth anniversary of the merger of the two South Carolina Conferences.

On Monday, June 5, 1972, the 107th and final session of the South Carolina Annual Conference (1866) met in Leonard Auditorium at Wofford College. Bishop Paul Hardin Jr., who had served as the bishop of both annual conferences since 1968 and of the 1785 Conference since 1960, led the last session. According to the Reverend John W. Curry's book *Passionate Journey*, Bishop Hardin read the same Scripture Bishop Osman C. Baker had read in April 1866 when he convened the first session of that Annual Conference. Reverend Curry read a historical statement about the 1866 Conference. The members approved some items of business and then approved a resolution transferring all of their members and property into the new annual conference that would be organized that evening. Their final act before adjourning sine die was to take up an offering for a hospital and church in Rhodesia.

It seemed symbolic in some way that the conference that had for so long been intertwined with Claflin University had its final session on the campus of another conference college. In remarks to the meeting of the South Carolina Conference Historical Society in the spring of 2022, Dr. A. V. Huff, the conference historian, noted the high emotion in the room. He noted that he and some other members of the 1785 conference had attended to witness the historic moment that had been in the works for more than thirty years.

At 2:00 that afternoon, the 1785 Conference met at Spartanburg Memorial Auditorium for its final session. It also approved similar resolutions transferring its members and property to the new annual conference. Following some other final remarks and recognitions, the 1785 Conference adjourned sine die.

At 7:30 that evening, the conferences met together in Spartanburg Memorial Auditorium for a service of worship and act of unification of the two conferences. Representatives of the youth, laity, clergy, and Women's Society of Christian Service joined in the litany of union. At the end, members of both conferences joined in stating, "We are united in Christ. We are united in The United Methodist Church. Now we are united in the South Carolina Annual Conference. We pledge our love and loyalty. Amen."

Hardin then declared "the Conference of '85 and the Conference of '66 to be united in a new annual conference to be called the South Carolina Annual Conference of the United Methodist Church."

Union had been accomplished, but the hard work was not over. The new conference had to live into the promises that its Plan of Union had made. And while the denomination and the leaders who had brought about the merger had intended for it to be just that, a merger, at times it may have seemed much more like an absorption. The 1866 Conference had been much smaller, and it would have been very easy for all the Black members of the new conference to have lost all the leadership positions that they had exercised in the former 1866 Conference. Financial and leadership concerns had been some of the biggest obstacles to merger.

Curry's book noted one of these financial questions arose on the floor of the 1785 conference, and it was specifically about the different pension rates paid in the two conferences. However, the former 1866 conference had worked hard to increase its pension fund, and as a result, the pension rate after merger was higher than in either conference before merger.

Another challenge that the new conference faced was leadership. Hardin finished his third quadrennium and retired in 1972, leaving a new bishop, Edward L. Tullis, to lead the new conference. Curry noted that the members of the 1866 conference had been nervous about Hardin, but "his clearness of vision, brotherly kindness, and skill in presiding soon dispelled this uneasiness." Bishop Tullis likewise worked hard to earn the trust of the conference, particularly by visiting Black churches, attending clergy funerals, and by learning clergy members' names.

An adjourned session of the conference met in October to elect leadership for conference boards and commissions. On Wednesday, October 4, the conference elected members of all conference councils, boards, commissions, and committees, based on the nominations that came from the Committee on Nominations.

These groups then met to select their officers.

While the Plan of Union called for ensuring leadership opportunities for members of both former conferences for several quadrennia, when the elections took place, all of the conference boards had elected chairs from the former 1785 conference. According to Curry's history, the bishop gently but firmly encouraged them to reconsider. The conference minutes show the conference directed the boards to meet again within thirty days following the adjournment of the conference to elect officers and offered guidance from the continuing Committee on Merger. That stumbling point could have eroded trust in the Plan of Union, but the boards and commissions responded positively, and eight of them, including the Conference Board of Trustees, Council on Ministries, Board of Pensions, and the Committee on Resolutions and Appeals, all elected chairs from the former 1866 conference.

The 1972 merger initially only affected the conference-level organizations. The eleven districts from the 1785 conference and the four districts from the 1866 conference continued for two more years. In 1974, the district lines were redrawn to create twelve new districts. While the bishop always had the right to choose their superintendents, the continuing merger committee recommended that four of the superintendents come from the former 1866 conference. The new districts meant that White congregations would have Black district superintendents, and vice versa. Curry's book noted that it meant in some cases a congregation that a dozen years before would not have welcomed Black worshipers would be welcoming a Black clergy person to preside over their charge conferences. It would also mean a Black parsonage family might be living in a largely White neighborhood.

The merger of the two South Carolina conferences in June 1972 was the result of work begun in 1939, but it left unresolved questions that have taken years to untangle. Merger took years to become effective and relied on building new relationships among clergy and laity.

For fifty years, South Carolina Methodists have tried to live into those promises made in the spring and summer of 1972.

# Chapter 43

## South Carolina Methodism Enters the Seventies

While the merger of the two South Carolina Conferences became effective in June 1972, true merger would be an ongoing process.

By May 1973, some of the details were still being discussed. One of those involved the number of districts the new conference would include, and perhaps most significantly, the district superintendent's role. The merger plan called for combining the eleven districts of the 1785 conference and the four districts of the 1866 conference into twelve new districts by 1974.

Readers of the *Advocate* in May 1973 saw two proposed maps. A task force came up with one map that reflected the direction in the plan of union, placing around fifty to fifty-five charges in each district. However, the task force also submitted a second map proposing fourteen districts of around forty charges each.

The *Advocate's* editorial found strong arguments for each map:

> If these persons of essential leadership responsibility are to continue to fulfill the duties of this office as presently envisioned, primarily, that of an administrator spending much time at the desk or on the road going from charge to charge, it is our judgment that 12 districts are sufficient. If, on the other hand, we are to grasp the emerging role of the superintendent as that of an enabler, counselor, and senior elder with responsibility for continuing education, training, and consultation, a greater number of districts is a must.

To expect the superintendent to be a leader rather than an administrator required smaller districts.

The conference's new bishop, Edward L. Tullis, continued the practice of his predecessor in writing a weekly column detailing his activities. One week he wrote about attending the Council of Bishops meeting where they held their first-ever open-to-the-public session. "Openness is the word for the day, and I believe this practice of an open meeting will become a part of our regular sessions," the bishop wrote. He also noted the privilege of attending the National Symphony Orchestra's performance of Mahler's Resurrection symphony, which he felt especially appropriate during the Easter season.

Another of the bishop's columns noted several events that took place at the conference's colleges in April and May. The new bishop was busy giving commencement addresses, which he did at Columbia College on May 4 and at Claflin University on May 14. He also noted a visit to Candler to meet the South Carolina students there, an event organized by Dr. Roger Gramling, who was then a student. And, on April 12, Tullis took part in the installation of Dr. Joab Lesesne as Wofford's ninth president.

The *Advocate* printed a summary of Lesesne's inaugural address, in which the new president both defended academic freedom as practiced at Wofford and called for strengthened ties with the church:

> I believe one of the most important contributions a church-related college can make to the church is to put forth forcefully the informed Christian alternative in the world of competing ideals .... Students who attend Wofford will leave to live in a pluralistic world. In America, religious and philosophical creeds are legion. Our students must be helped to develop their faith to live in that world, a faith which understands diversity and a faith that has had the fullest opportunity to mature.

The issues that South Carolina Methodists struggled with in the 1970s remain with us today.

# Chapter 44

## Susanna Wesley: Mother of Methodism

The year 2019 marked the 350th birthday of Susanna Wesley, the mother of John and Charles Wesley, who many regard as the mother of Methodism.

What do we know about her? She was born in London on January 20, 1669, the twenty-fifth child of Rev. Samuel Annesley, who himself was one of the leading dissenting (I'd interpret this as Puritan) ministers in London during the reign of King Charles II. Samuel Annesley sometimes got in trouble for not holding to the teachings of the established church, something his grandson perhaps inherited.

Susanna married Samuel Wesley, an Anglican priest who had studied at Oxford. They lived in London, and later in South Ormsby, and finally, in 1697, they settled in Epworth, where Samuel Wesley would remain the rector for thirty-nine years.

The life of an Anglican clergyman was not one of wealth, and having nineteen children—though nearly half of them did not survive infancy—added to their financial burden. Susanna was primarily responsible for her children's education and all of them, seven daughters and three sons, received a very good classical education. The siblings were in school for six hours a day from the time they were five years old. She also spent some time each week with each child individually, which had a memorable effect on each of them.

Fires—which were all too common in the days of wooden structures, cooking over an open hearth, and no organized fire departments or hydrants—struck the Wesley family several times. John Wesley's rescue from the burning Epworth rectory as a small child is a famous story in Methodism, but it was not the first fire to put pressure on the family. With so many children to care for, after the 1709 fire, Susanna and Samuel had to send their children to live with other families, which disrupted their educational routines. When they finally had restored their circumstances in the rectory, almost two years later, Susanna found her children had picked up some bad habits.

Much of what Susanna did with her children was as much improvised as it was intentional, but her improvisations turned out to have had a profound impact on her children, and perhaps even on the future of Methodism. During one of Samuel's extended absences, his replacement in the Epworth pulpit wasn't particularly inspiring. As an improvisation, Susanna took to holding religious services on Sunday afternoons for the children, often reading one of her father's or husband's sermons from the file. When friends and neighbors found this out, they asked to come, and soon more people were attending her improvised service than the parish church service.

The religious conversion of John and Charles through the Holy Club at Oxford may have perplexed Susanna, but her own experience of salvation, according to historian Maldwyn Edwards, helped her to accept it.

After Samuel's death in 1735, and after John and Charles' oldest brother Samuel Jr.'s death in 1739, she wound up living at the Foundery in London and was thus for several years at the center of the fledgling Methodist movement. It was thanks to her influence, after hearing one of the early lay preachers, that John was moved to agree that lay preachers could be valuable in spreading the Gospel. That perhaps made Methodism grow faster in England than it would have otherwise.

Susanna died in London on July 30, 1742, with her family gathered around her.

# Chapter 45

## Charles Wesley: O For a Thousand Hymns?

Charles Wesley labored alongside his older brother John in the Methodist movement, providing leadership in the organization at several critical points.

Charles Wesley was born on December 18, 1707, at Epworth, and like his siblings, received his early education from his mother, Susanna. In 1716, he entered the Westminster School in London, and later became a King's Scholar, which meant his family was no longer responsible for his upkeep. Continuing his education, he went to Christ Church College of Oxford, which John had just left.

At Oxford, Charles began to spend time in personal devotion and founded the Holy Club. It grew, and when John returned to Oxford the next year, he assumed leadership of the Holy Club. Largely at John's insistence, Charles was ordained to the Anglican priesthood, and he traveled with John to Georgia to serve as a secretary to General James Oglethorpe. The experience did not go well for either Wesley, as Charles was not suited for the assignment he took. He left Georgia within a year, partly to carry some messages back to England, but partly for health reasons. Back in England, he expressed no desire to return, and after recovering from a serious illness, connected with a Moravian missionary. Thus began the connection between the Wesleys and the Moravians, a relationship that brought a new ingredient into their faith.

Charles had his conversion experience on May 21, 1738, three days before his brother's Aldersgate experience.

The next decades were busy ones for both Wesleys. Charles preached in the churches of London that welcomed him, but gradually, those became fewer. He visited prisoners and began preaching in the fields. Unlike his brother, Charles had a happy marriage. He married in 1749 and settled in Bristol, in the west of England. As a result, he stopped much of his traveling on behalf of the church. This may have been one of the reasons his marriage was a happy one, though his lack of availability for traveling was a source of frustration for John. The older brother, however, was not exactly one to be giving advice on maintaining a happy home, as we know. It is worth noting that Methodism grew in Bristol and in the area around it because of Charles' presence there.

Charles and his family did move to London in 1771, where he took a more active role in the Methodist movement. The musical education of his two sons prompted the move more than any desire to further the work of the church, but he did wind up staying busy in the church's work.

Though often in John's shadow in the Methodist movement's leadership, Charles was an essential force in early Methodism. He was disappointed when John decided to ordain clergy for work in the American church and remained an Anglican all his life.

Of course, we know Charles best as the hymnodist of the faith, and not just the Methodist faith. He wrote more than 6,000 hymns in his life, and a few of them are the most prominent in today's Methodist Church. Millions of Christians around the world sing his hymns even if they only go to church on Christmas and Easter, because he wrote "Hark the Herald Angels Sing" and "Christ the Lord is Risen Today." He also wrote "O For a Thousand Tongues to Sing" and "Love Divine, All Loves Excelling" among many, many more.

# Chapter 46

## The Women in John Wesley's Life

Recently I wrote about Susanna Wesley, the mother of John Wesley and Charles Wesley. Some students of Methodism have referred to Susanna as the "Mother of Methodism" because of the influence she had on John, both as a boy and as a young clergyman.

Susanna was not the only woman who was a part of John Wesley's life or who had an influence on the early Methodist movement. However, from most accounts, John Wesley had several troubled personal relationships with women.

While he was serving in Georgia, he fell in love with a young woman named Sophia Hopkey. According to a recent book on Wesley's time in Georgia, the young priest admired Hopkey's simple faith. But Wesley was torn between his desire to serve the people who he was sent to serve and his love for Sophy. He considered proposing marriage, but never actually did. Sophy got tired of waiting and agreed to marry someone else. Following this, Wesley believed her devotion to her faith had fallen away and suggested she not take Communion. When she came to take Communion anyway, he refused to serve her, and that caused a scandal in the Georgia colony. Hopkey's uncle was the chief magistrate in Savannah, which meant Wesley may have offended the wrong family. Historian Geordan Hammond notes in his book *John Wesley in America* that Wesley had several close friendships with women in Georgia and that also caused some of his difficulties there.

Following the incident with Sophia Hopkey, Wesley returned abruptly to England.

After his Aldersgate experience, Wesley began traveling throughout Britain to preach wherever he could, and he established societies in various parts of the country. He developed friendships and mentorships in many places, often with women. One of those was Grace Murray, a widow who was a class leader in one of the societies. Charles Wesley did not think John should marry Grace, partly because he believed her to be beneath John in social status, but also because he believed it would cause friction in the Methodist societies for him to marry one of his followers. Grace ultimately married someone else, and Charles performed the ceremony.

Finally, in 1751, John Wesley married Mary Vazeille, a well-to-do widow with four children. However, he did not cease traveling or corresponding with the women in the various Methodist societies, which caused friction. Molly, as she was known, had a temper, and she and John said plenty of not-so-nice things to and about each other. When he left for a tour of Ireland in 1758, Molly wrote that John said, "I hope I shall see your wicked face no more." Finally, in 1771, Molly left John for good. In his diary, he wrote "For what cause I know not to this day, [my wife] set out for Newcastle purposing 'never to return.' I did not leave her: I did not send her away: I will not call her back.'" When Mary died in 1781, he was not informed in time to attend her burial.

Given the demands placed on his time by nurturing the growing Methodist movement, John probably should never have married. But that's not to say he disapproved of women serving in the church, for after some of his women class leaders began to cross the line into preaching, and were able to justify it, he began to allow women to serve as lay preachers in the societies.

Many clergy even today struggle with how to balance their ministry and their responsibilities to their families, and perhaps it's good for all of us to recognize there's nothing new in that.

# Section 5

## Communities

While leaders, historical events, and conference institutions are all important, the growth and development of local churches in South Carolina helps tie individual Methodists to the larger connection. Again, I have not covered every community, and I have plenty more research and writing to do in the future to cover more communities in the state. Often these writings were based on stories published in the Advocate when annual conference met in that community.

# Chapter 47

## Methodism in Charleston

Many South Carolinians call it the "Holy City," but it's safe to say Charleston has had a long and complicated relationship with Methodism. Sometimes supporting the church's growth and sometimes finding its doctrines in opposition to the prevailing culture, Charleston has been a part of South Carolina Methodism's story since before there was a Methodist church.

Charleston can claim a connection to early Methodism that very few places in North America can match. John Wesley visited the Holy City on a few occasions while he was serving in Georgia. According to Francis Asbury Mood's *Methodism in Charleston*, John and Charles Wesley arrived in Charleston on July 31, 1736, barely six months after his arrival in Georgia. He was there to visit Rev. Alexander Garden, who was the rector of St. Philip's Church and the representative of the Anglican Bishop of London.

Reverend Garden invited John Wesley to preach in St. Philip's, which Wesley did on Sunday, August 1, to about 300 parishioners. At this service, Wesley encountered several enslaved persons among the worshippers, which had a profound effect on him. The next day, Mood notes that Wesley paid a call on the governor, who in 1736 would have been Thomas Broughton. He then returned to Savannah, starting out on foot because he could find no other passage available. Charles Wesley was soon to leave Savannah, having found serving as Governor Oglethorpe's secretary not in keeping with his skills.

John Wesley made two more trips to Charleston, once to visit with Reverend Garden to ask the rector of St. Philip's to help put an end to someone in Georgia marrying his parishioners without going through proper procedures. Mood does not mention the other reason Wesley visited—to have his *Collection of Psalms and Hymns* printed at the Lewis Timothy print shop on King Street. Wesley's final visit to Charleston was after he abruptly left Georgia in late 1737 on his way back to England.

Mood notes that George Whitfield, who was an early collaborator in ministry with Wesley, also visited several times in Charleston, but after an early visit, his street preaching offended Reverend Garden, who had him suspended from the ministry. Whitfield took to other pulpits to spread his message. One of Wesley's ministers visited Charleston in the 1770s but did not leave much of a record of his presence.

After the 1784 Christmas Conference, Bishop Francis Asbury journeyed to Charleston, with Rev. Jesse Lee and Rev. Henry Willis helping him set up preaching places. Reverend Willis found a deserted Baptist meeting house on the west side of Church Street between Water and Tradd streets and restored it for services. Bishop Asbury himself visited both St. Philip's and the Circular Congregational Church as he familiarized himself with religion in Charleston. After Bishop Asbury left in March, Reverend Willis stayed behind, and at the next conference in the spring, Charleston Circuit was established. The Methodists continued to worship in the borrowed meeting house for a few months, but one Sunday, they found their benches in the street and the doors locked. The congregation was a bit itinerant until they secured a lot in early 1786, where they built a structure by mid-1787. The lot, on Cumberland Street between Meeting and Church, was the first permanent Methodist church in Charleston. Charlestonians may be able to claim visits from John Wesley, but they were not always as kind to his successors. While Methodism took root in Charleston in the 1780s and grew in the 1790s, it was not without opposition and even persecution.

With the completion of the Cumberland Street Church, the first meeting of the South Carolina Annual Conference was held in Charleston in 1787. The next year, when Annual Conference again met at the church, a mob attacked outside during the Sunday morning service. The women of the church were so frightened that many of them escaped out the church's windows. Later that night, protesters threw bricks and rocks at the church while Bishop Asbury was preaching. The next year, the newspaper denounced Bishop Thomas Coke when he visited the Holy City.

Why all this opposition to early Methodists? Perhaps it was their antislavery position, or that they had more African-American members than White members in some early years. Perhaps it was their evangelical zeal that put off the

Charlestonians, who were fairly low key in their religious practice. In any event, as long as the Methodists held on to their opposition to slavery, they found condemnation among White Charleston society.

Those early Methodists faced other internal challenges. When Bishop Coke arrived for the 1791 Conference, he brought with him Rev. William Hammett, who had been working among Methodists in the British West Indies. His enthusiastic preaching wowed the Methodists of Charleston, and they demanded that Bishop Asbury appoint him to Charleston. However, Bishop Asbury had already decided on the appointments and was unwilling to budge.

Hammett, who was probably not the first clergyman to be disappointed with his appointment, and certainly not the last, protested. He went further than most clergy and took his protests to the newspapers. He then led about half of the aggrieved members of the Cumberland Street church out to form a new congregation, calling themselves "Primitive Methodists." His members acquired property on Hasell Street and took the name Trinity, and the deed made the church Hammett's personal property (a practice that the denomination wisely doesn't permit).

Hammett preached there until his death in 1813. The Primitive Methodists eventually spun off a second congregation, which became St. James.

Although wounded by the loss of so many members, Cumberland, sometimes called the Blue Meeting House, continued, and looked in 1793 to start a second Charleston congregation. They acquired land for a cemetery on which they also planned to build a church, and as soon as they raised 300 pounds, they began construction on what became Bethel.

The "regular" Methodists continued to face criticism and attacks from Charleston society, and the protests increased in force and volume during the early nineteenth century. Finally, the church abandoned its long-held antislavery positions, choosing the path of growth in the South over Wesley's teachings. The attacks gradually stopped.

Black Methodists grew increasingly frustrated with the White leadership of the local congregations. While the enslaved Methodists had class leaders and some control over finances in the class groups, a movement was under way to take that away. Given their numbers, it's likely the Black classes had deeper coffers. When the White leadership took away that financial control, many of the African-American members withdrew to form a new congregation and denomination. That loss of membership marked a momentous change in the antebellum Methodist church in Charleston.

After Hammett's death, Trinity Church eventually came back into the fold, though they had to fight off a minister to whom Hammett had willed the church who tried to take the congregation back into the Episcopal Church. In 1816, Trinity returned to the Methodist Episcopal Church. The second church started by the Primitive Methodists, St. James, eventually became Spring Street Church.

Not long after the Hammett schism, the remaining members of the original congregation, Cumberland, helped start a second congregation, which became Bethel. That church, which was first built in 1797, served its congregation until the 1850s, when a new structure was built. The old structure, moved across the street and given to the congregation's Black membership, became Old Bethel, which is undoubtedly the oldest Methodist place of worship in continuous use in South Carolina.

Up until the 1840s, Methodist ministers were appointed to Charleston and collectively served all of the churches in the city. In one announcement from 1837, seven different ministers preached at no less than fifteen services over the course of the week. The four congregations—Bethel, Trinity, Cumberland, and St. James/Spring Street—each had three Sunday services, morning, afternoon, and night. A weeknight service rotated between Bethel, Trinity, and Cumberland on Tuesday, Wednesday, and Friday night.

Given the small geographic size of the Charleston peninsula, no Methodist in the Holy City had an excuse not to attend a worship service at some time each week.

During the Civil War, the Spring Street Church was used as a Confederate medical storehouse, and at the end of the war, the federal army seized it and gave it to the Northern missionary conference for the use of Charleston's freedmen. The property was returned on the orders of President Andrew Johnson in 1868.

At the conclusion of the Civil War in 1865, Charleston's Methodists worshipped at four churches—Bethel, Trinity, Cumberland, and Spring Street. About 500 White Methodists were on the rolls of those three churches, according to the minutes of the conference held in 1866. Outside of Charleston proper, another 1,000 White and 700 African-American Methodists were part of the Summerville, Cooper River, Walterboro, Black Swamp, and Hardeeville circuits, and the Summerville Station.

Charleston Methodism had been strongly biracial before the Civil War, but with emancipation, the Black members of the congregations withdrew. The northern branch of the Methodist Episcopal Church organized a new annual conference, and disagreements over control over church property and where

Black Methodists would worship were coming to a head. At a meeting at Trinity Church, the Reverend T. Willard Lewis rose and shouted, "Brothers and sisters, there will be no galleries in heaven, those who care to go with a church that makes no distinctions as to race or color, follow me to the Normal School at the corner of Beaufain and St. Philip Streets."

Many of those members helped organize the congregation that became called Old Bethel.

Annual Conference regularly met in Charleston, and on several occasions, the churches would submit items about their history for publication in the *Advocate*. By the end of the 1920s, five White Methodist congregations operated in and around Charleston: Bethel, Cumberland, North Charleston, Spring Street, and Trinity.

Charleston's twentieth-century growth would see Methodism expand beyond the historic center. As Charleston grew beyond the peninsula, the need for churches outside of downtown began to grow. However, one church has its roots in the antebellum era. Francis Asbury would have visited the Methodist society in Mount Pleasant on one of his many visits to Charleston. Around 1799, he helped organize that society. Later, in 1809, James Hibben donated land, and finally, around 1830, the congregation built a building. That structure lasted until after the Civil War. After a period apparently without a building, the members of the Hibben Church built a new structure between 1899 and 1901. That church remained in use until the 1950s, when the congregation moved to their current location. As Mount Pleasant grew, so did the congregation.

Charlestonians crossed the Ashley as well, and growth in the West Ashley area led to the organization of a new church in 1944. A core group met in the summer and fall of 1944, and a special charge conference in October with 125 charter members chose the name "John Wesley." They formed a building committee, and within two years, an educational building was opened. The church then prepared for building a sanctuary, which opened in July 1951. That sanctuary is still in use.

Of course, many other congregations in and around the Holy City have grown up and contributed to Methodism's story in South Carolina.

# Chapter 48

## Cokesbury, the Methodist Town

Perhaps you've heard of Cokesbury—it's an especially Methodist name—but I'm not talking about the publishing house. I'm talking about the village in Greenwood County, South Carolina. That's correct; we have our very own Cokesbury right here in South Carolina.

I suppose you can be forgiven for having not heard of it. After all, it's not even an official town, but the government recognizes it as a census area, and as of 2000, the census counted some 279 people living there. Though it might be small, Cokesbury has a long history, and most of it is related to South Carolina Methodism.

In the 1820s, in perhaps an early real estate maneuver, the citizens of the nearby Methodist community called Tabernacle decided they wanted to move their town to higher, more pleasant ground. The Tabernacle Society had developed perhaps before 1788, making it a fairly early Methodist community. The town already had a school for boys, but they wanted both their town and their school to grow. They laid out a new village along a high ridge, with lots of some twenty to twenty-five acres, large enough for small farms, making it one of the state's earliest planned communities. At first they called their new town Mount Ariel, but in 1834, they changed the name to honor Bishops Thomas Coke and Francis Asbury.

In that same year, the annual conference decided it needed a preparatory-type school for boys, and it quickly decided to offer to purchase the Tabernacle Academy. It was named the Dougherty Manual Labor School, in honor of early clergyman George Dougherty, though it was commonly called the Cokesbury

Conference School almost from the beginning. Revs. William Wightman and William Capers, both future bishops, were on its first board of trustees. The village became a center of Methodism and education, and soon, the Cokesbury Methodist Church was built.

In addition to the school for boys, a Masonic Female College opened around 1854, and the village also had a school for children younger than age twelve. The Female College built a three-story Greek Revival building with a chapel on the second floor and recitation rooms on the first floor. The Female College operated in the building for some twenty years, at which point the conference purchased it and made it the home of the Cokesbury Conference School. The school was coeducational under Methodist operation from 1882 to 1918, at which point it became a public school. It reverted to Methodist hands in the 1950s, and most of Cokesbury became a National Historic District in 1970. More recently, it has been operated by the Cokesbury Historical and Recreational Commission.

Like many Upcountry towns, the residents of Cokesbury valued their idyllic, peaceful village and objected to the railroad coming to their community. That proved problematic to the community's growth after the Civil War. Growth shifted away from Cokesbury and toward Greenwood, which had become a railroad village.

When Greenwood County was created in 1897, with the city of Greenwood as its seat, Cokesbury's influence continued to decline. Greenwood's leaders encouraged Rev. Samuel Lander to move his college from Williamston to their city, and it opened there in 1903 as Lander College, where it retained its Methodist relationship until the 1940s.

# Chapter 49

## Methodism in Columbia

When Columbia was settled after the American Revolution, it was within the bounds of the old Santee Circuit. Rev. Isaac Smith was one of the earliest Methodist ministers to preach in Columbia, often holding services at the home of Colonel Thomas Taylor. Rev. John Harper, an Englishman ordained by John Wesley, sometimes preached in the Statehouse. Having located and acquired a home in Columbia in 1803, Harper, it appears, was instrumental in organizing a Methodist congregation. He deeded the lot on which the Washington Street Church was built. Very quickly the church became a station appointment.

Bishop Francis Asbury recounts several visits to Columbia in his journal. He notes arriving on a rainy November day and being welcomed into the home of Harper, where many people came to hear him preach. On a later trip in 1810, United States Senator John Taylor allowed Asbury to hold Annual Conference in his home. In December 1812, he reported, "I preached in the legislature chamber, and had the members for a part of my congregation."

The 1933 story "Columbia and Methodism," written by *Advocate* Editor the Reverend E. O. Watson, noted the role Washington Street Church had played in founding other congregations.

By 1848, Washington Street was crowded enough that another congregation became necessary, this one built on Marion Street. But some fifty years later, that church burned and was rebuilt on Main Street, and it has been known as Main Street Church ever since. The 1933 Upper South Carolina Conference met there.

A few blocks south, Greene Street Church began through the efforts of Rev. William Martin in 1879. The Whaley Street Church began in the Granby area around 1896. The author also noted, "Shandon was first organized in 1909 and its first church building located on Maple and Preston Streets was erected in 1910. This building was burned in 1914 and immediately rebuilt on the same site."

In 1931, Shandon moved to its present location at Devine and Millwood—though in what looks to be an amusing typo, the writer called it "Divine Street," an amusing address for a church. Churches at Brookland, organized around 1892, and College Place, in 1913, continue the story.

The story of Methodism in Columbia in 1933 was nowhere near complete. Because it was a different conference, the Black churches in Columbia didn't make it into the 1933 story. Columbia College's growth and development from 1854 to the present day, the establishment and growth of Epworth Children's Home, and the *Advocate* itself are other Methodist institutions that contribute to the story of Methodism in the area and in the state.

Less than thirty years after that story was written, after the merger of the Upper South Carolina and South Carolina conferences, the Southeastern Jurisdiction made Columbia the seat of a bishop, and so in 1960, the Columbia Area was born.

Now most Methodists in South Carolina who sit on any conference board or commission have made the trip to the United Methodist Center on Colonial Drive.

# Chapter 50

## Early Methodism in Georgetown

Methodism made it to Georgetown County pretty quickly, as many of Bishop Francis Asbury's trips to South Carolina brought him to Georgetown and Horry counties.

Asbury reached Georgetown on March 10, 1785, a little more than two months after the Christmas Conference in Baltimore where the Methodist Episcopal Church was organized. In January 1786, he was back. He writes that he preached twice to about eighty people each time in Georgetown on Saturday, January 7. He wrote, "This is a poor place for religion." But in a year, things must have changed. On March 15, 1787, he wrote that "the scene was greatly changed, almost the whole town came together to hear the word of the Lord."

Since he had to visit each conference every year, Asbury tended to spend the winter months in South Carolina. A February 1791 visit left him in a bad mood. It rained, and he said that he preached a plain, searching sermon, and some felt the word. In the afternoon, he preached again, but the wicked youths were playing without and inattention prevailed among those within.

He spent Christmas 1795 in Horry and Georgetown counties, spending Christmas Eve in Kingston (Conway) and traveling to Georgetown on Christmas Day. He spent a few days there, noting that the dancing and playhouses that had previously been there were gone, but that ten years' work had not yet produced much.

On his way from Georgetown to Charleston that year, Asbury noted the prevalence of slavery on the rice plantations. He said, "Here are the rich, the rice, and the slaves, the last is awful to me." A year later, when he was back in Georgetown

County, he noted the society had about one hundred Black members but only eight or ten Whites. "Our discipline is too strict," he observed. I think he meant it was too strict for White folks.

In his 1802 visit, he expressed some pride in the transformation of Methodism in the area around Georgetown. "What South Carolina was to Methodism when I first came to Georgetown, I know, and what it is now, I know, but what may it be thirty years hence?" The bishop had his eye on the future. The weather that January, he said, was like April.

His visits to Georgetown in the 1800s saw him making more comments about the demographics of the church—it was largely made up of enslaved women and men. Bishop Asbury urged slaveholding Methodists to teach their slaves to read so they could better understand the gospel.

His last visit was New Year's 1813. By then he said, after twenty-nine years of work here, he felt at home. He stayed a few days, catching up on his correspondence. He noted the society's membership was about 1,000 Black people and one hundred White people—mostly women.

"The men kill themselves with strong drink before we can get at them," he wrote.

The denomination may have surrendered its opposition to slavery, but it did not abandon the enslaved. Much of the South Carolina Conference's missionary work in the nineteenth century was on plantations. James L. Belin was one of those missionary ministers.

Belin served on the Cooper River, Waccamaw, and Black Swamp circuits, and in the late 1830s, he helped form the Waccamaw Neck Mission. He was associated with that mission to the slaves on Waccamaw Neck until his death in November 1859. He led the way in preaching to Black members, starting by 1819 on the Springfield and Brookgreen plantations. He devoted much of the energy of his later years to ministering to the slave population of the area.

At his death, he left almost all of his property to that work.

# Chapter 51

## The Beginning of Methodism in Greenville

The thrilling and inspiring story of Methodism in Greenville should give assurance to all that Methodism has not lost her power, and that God is still with his church and blessing it."

So began Monroe Pickens's seven-page history of Greenville Methodism in the October 30, 1941, *Advocate*. For the eighth time, Annual Conference was meeting in Greenville, having met at Buncombe Street in 1859, 1874, 1882, 1901, 1916, and 1932, and at St. Paul's in 1927. Pickens's story gave those attending conference some information about a place with which they were no doubt familiar.

Pickens continued:

> We cannot fix a definite date on which Methodism was introduced into Greenville, but it is certain that the pioneer Methodist circuit riders commenced their work here during the closing years of the eighteenth century. Methodist congregations were organized, and at an early date a number of these congregations formed the old Greenville Circuit, and regular pastors were assigned to it. These pastors were not slow in establishing their work, and with the help of local preachers soon entered new fields, one of these being Pleasantburg village, now Greenville, and by 1832 preaching was held regularly in the county courthouse.

The beginning of recorded Greenville Methodism dates to 1832, when on the eleventh day of October, Vardry McBee deeded a lot on Coffee Street, near the village of Greenville, "for the promotion of religious worship in order that a suitable church may be erected for the Methodist denomination of professors to assemble."

The congregation was organized in 1834 with six members. The services probably continued in the courthouse until 1836, when a church was erected on Coffee Street. After 1872, the building was made a residence and did good service until 1941 when it was torn down.

The church became a station appointment in 1841, with Rev. William P. Mouzon as pastor. At the end of the first year, eighty-one names were on the register, with members in three classes. Prayer meetings were held on Monday evening and love feasts were held quarterly. A class of Black members, whose names and numbers were not given in the records, met on Sunday afternoons, and the pastor preached at this meeting. The church continued to grow, building new facilities in the 1870s.

In 1891, Dr. J. A. Clifton held preaching services in the home of Mr. A. H. Cureton in the city's "West End," then in a large room in the Greenville Hotel, and finally in a vacant storeroom. About one hundred attended these services, and thus Rev. R. H. Jones was appointed to form a new congregation. On December 19, 1891, St. Paul was organized, with some fifty members coming from the Greenville Charge, which was renamed Buncombe Street. St. Paul's congregation bought a lot on Green Avenue and built a chapel, which served the congregation until 1910.

Readers who know their South Carolina history will recall that the textile industry began a period of serious growth in the 1880s and 1890s, and the Piedmont Southeast was the center of the southern textile industry. So it should come as no shock that Greenville saw growth in mill community churches in the last decade of the nineteenth century. Both Bethel and Buncombe Street had a hand in organizing these new congregations. The church at Samson-Poe started around 1896, with the clergyman in charge appearing on the rolls as a member of Buncombe Street's quarterly conference. That evolved into the Greenville City Mission by 1900, and mission status indicated that the church or churches were not fully self-sustaining but were an outreach ministry of the conference. A congregation evolved on Highland Avenue around this same time, which later became Hampton Avenue. Bethel helped organize the church at Brandon in 1901.

In the next decade, five different congregations emerged in Greenville, including Choice Street, Monaghan, Mills Mill, Woodside, and Union Bleachery, which later became St. John. By the end of 1910, Greenville had nine White

Methodist congregations. Dunean, Judson, and Poinsett were organized in the next decade. Judson got its start in a mill cottage before later moving to the mill hall. Often, textile companies helped build church buildings or helped pay for expansions, including some at Bethel. In the third decade of mill church growth in Greenville, several of these congregations built nice brick churches, such as Woodside, which had a seating capacity of 300, with 200 more in adjacent Sunday school rooms. That building cost more than $20,000. In the 1920s, the Poe Mill spent some $50,000 on that church. By the early 1920s, the area had fifteen congregations with 4,000 members. Some of these congregations, including Duncan Chapel and Poinsett, disappeared in the 1920s.

In his 1941 *Advocate* story "Methodism in Greenville," Monroe Pickens reported that Greenville had twelve congregations, four parsonages, and close to 7,000 members in those White churches. Pickens is, of course, silent on the experience of Greenville's Black Methodists, but thanks to the work of Fred W. Bostic, we know a good deal about the history of John Wesley Church in Greenville. His 2006 history of the church covers its founding by Rev. James Rosemond, a pioneering clergyman in the 1866 conference who founded dozens of congregations in the Upcountry. Originally called Silver Hill (the same name as Spartanburg's church), Rev. Rosemond was able to acquire land for the church at the corner of Choice and Cleveland streets in 1866. The current John Wesley Church was started in 1899 and dedicated in 1903 at the corner of Court and Falls streets.

# Chapter 52

## Early Methodism in Spartanburg

On one of his 1788 visits to the Spartanburg area, Bishop Francis Asbury wrote in his journal, "Our Friends here on Tyger River are much alive to God, and have built a good chapel." Three older congregations, Liberty northeast of Spartanburg, Shiloh in Inman, and Sharon near Reidville all have their roots in the late eighteenth or early nineteenth century. Liberty pre-dates the first annual conference in South Carolina and made a traditional evolution from brush arbor to log structure to frame church. It has served as something of a focal point in the Liberty community for centuries.

Church legend holds that famed preacher Lorenzo Dow helped organize Sharon United Methodist Church, which was called Leonard's Meeting House, as it was founded by the Leonard family. Lorenzo Dow was perhaps not the kind of fellow you'd want to invite to dinner—he was wild, unkempt, did not practice much in the way of personal hygiene, and was very enthusiastic in his preaching. However, during the Second Great Awakening of the early nineteenth century, he was one of the most influential preachers in America. Stories say that he could hold the attention of a crowd of 10,000, and his autobiography was one of the most popular books in America.

One very old church structure that is no longer an active congregation is Shiloh, near Inman. The church was built between 1825 and 1831, though the congregation is older than that. The church and pews were built without nails. It was discontinued as a regular preaching place around 1912 when most of the people moved from the countryside around it into Inman, but it's still maintained and there are two services a year there—Homecoming in May and a watch night service at New Year's—as well as occasional weddings. It is a great example of what an antebellum church would have looked like.

We're all familiar with the stories of camp meetings, and many congregations around the state have their roots in camp meeting sites. Spartanburg's Cannon's Camp Ground is one such church. In the history of their congregation, there's a description of a Cannon's camp meeting. The undated letter from an attendee notes that the camp meeting was one of the biggest events of the year in Spartanburg from the 1830s to the early 1900s. Always held in late summer to early fall, when the daytime temperatures had dropped somewhat but before the nights were too cool for sleeping outside, the revivals attracted attendees from all over the Upcountry. Services at Cannon's were held five times a day, with time for breakfast, a large lunch and dinner, and plenty of time to sit around and visit with friends that they saw infrequently.

The village of Spartanburg received its legislative charter in 1831, and some six years later, the Methodists organized the first church within the city. That church eventually took the name Central, and it became a station appointment by 1850. One of its trustees was a local pastor named Benjamin Wofford, who had ceased the traveling ministry in 1820 to manage his wealthy wife's property. When he died in 1850, he left $100,000 to found a college in his native county to be under the control of the Methodist Conference. The trustees he named met at Central in April 1851 and named the college for its benefactor.

Central would help give birth to the second Methodist congregation in the community when one of its members, Mrs. Electa Button Leverton, invited friends to a class meeting in her home. That class meeting soon grew into a congregation that was first a mission church and later a free-standing one that took the name Bethel. As happened in nearby Greenville, the growth of textile mills in Spartanburg gave rise to a number of mill churches, including Duncan Memorial in the Spartan Mills community.

There are obviously many more churches with long histories, including Silver Hill Memorial, one of many churches founded by Rev. James Rosemond after emancipation, which has been a beacon to Black Methodists in Spartanburg for more than 150 years.

# Chapter 53

## Early Methodism in York County

A series of articles in 1908 talked about some of the early history of Methodism in York County, and they came from an address delivered at the fiftieth anniversary of Rock Hill Methodism in 1856. The articles featured the life and work of Rev. William Gassaway, a Virginia native who ended up in York County as a young man. There he felt God's call and made his confession to a Presbyterian clergyman, mostly because he couldn't find any other clergy in the area. He wound up in the Methodist Church and joined the conference in 1788. He was an itinerant for close to twenty-six years—quite a stretch in that era. In 1809, Gassaway hosted a visit by Bishop Francis Asbury when the pioneer bishop was traveling through York County on his way to meet the South Carolina Conference. A few years later, Gassaway decided to relocate, over Asbury's protests, but the clergyman had a family to support. It was hard for clergy to have families in that era, a sentiment Asbury expressed when he supposedly claimed that "the women and the devil are getting all of my preachers!"

It was also in an 1812 visit in York County, according to his journal, that Asbury arrived at some notable brethren's home after a cold December ride and noted "brandy and the Bible were both handed me; one was enough, I took but one." Asbury doesn't say which. Presumably, as a bishop, he had a Bible.

Gassaway and Rev. Joseph Holmes organized Trinity, York, the oldest Methodist church in York County, in 1824. They held the first Sunday school there in 1826. Gassaway remained involved with Trinity until his death in 1833, and so he is considered the pioneer of Methodism in York County. The church continued to grow, and of course as the new town of Rock Hill grew, Methodism took root there. The church that eventually became St. John's got its start in 1856, moving twice before building its current sanctuary in the mid-1920s. Articles about the history of St. John's and other Methodist congregations around Rock Hill in 1926 appeared in the *Advocate* in advance of the 1926 session of the Upper South Carolina Conference, which St. John's hosted. St. John's was initially part of the Rock Hill Circuit but had long since become a station appointment. Other churches on that circuit included Mount Holly, Friendship, Antioch, and Catawba. Mount Holly had 285 members "and the most progressive and cooperative membership to be found anywhere." The circuit as a whole had more than 500 members.

Besides the churches on the Rock Hill Circuit, the *Advocate* ran pictures of the Park Methodist Church on Jones Avenue and the Ogden Church, a rural church that was less than three years old.

Of course, Methodism continued to grow and influence life in York County well after 1926, but the stories of these churches show what a good foundation the church has in the area.

# Section 6

## Resources

These are resources that the Conference Archives has available for local churches and other researchers. Some are online, and some are publications that may be in a local library that will help you put your own church history into context. The archives has made clergy directories and conference journals available online, as well as the clergy photographs from those directories.

# Chapter 54

## Histories of the Conference

With nearly 240 years of history in South Carolina Methodism, it's not surprising that several writers have published books about the conference. It may be more noteworthy to consider how few have actually been written.

Three older works put much of their emphasis on Methodism in the Palmetto State in the nineteenth century. That's mostly because one, *The History of Methodism in South Carolina*, appeared in 1883, and the other, *Early Methodism in the Carolinas*, was published in 1897. These two books are not especially light reads. The first, by Rev. A. M. Shipp, Wofford's former president and a clergy member of the conference, is 648 pages long, and the second, by Rev. Abel M. Chreitzberg, was about 364 pages. Both books are heavy on biography, with short sketches of ministers and quotes from their journals. Each also goes into considerable detail about the organization of circuits and the proceedings of annual conferences and circuit quarterly conferences. The strength of both of these books is in the sheer volume of data they have amassed. The weakness is that, except for the subheadings in Chreitzberg's book, they lack any index. That makes it a little hard to find information about specific circuits or individuals. More importantly, though they contain a lot of data, they don't always tell stories, and they definitely don't tell a lot of stories of average Methodists. These types of books often try to avoid controversy, and of course, they are largely about the White church and reflect the attitudes of post-Civil War White South Carolinians. Any mention of Black Methodism is largely through the eyes of the missionaries to the enslaved persons.

The third of these three older books, the *History of South Carolina Methodism*, was published in 1952 by Rev. Albert D. Betts. It is also a fairly involved recitation of year-to-year events at annual conferences, to the point of reprinting the appointments and summarizing the actions. That can be useful as it can keep a researcher from having to review the entire conference journal. But, it doesn't make for interesting reading. It's more than 500 pages and does have a rudimentary index. Betts also covers the post-Civil War and early twentieth-century years and does talk about women's work while largely ignoring the Black church.

Other more recent books fill in some of the gaps in these earlier histories. *Steps Along the Way*, by Rev. Warren M. Jenkins, is a history of the 1866 Conference and the growth of Black Methodism in the state. Published in 1967, it has some of the same qualities as the Betts book in that it recounts a lot of the action at conference. Jenkins's book, because it looks at subjects ignored by the White conference histories, is especially valuable for researchers who are looking at Black church history.

*Passionate Journey*, by Rev. John W. Curry, was published in 1980, and it covers the history of the 1866 Conference as the merger with the 1785 Conference took place. It has a lot of lists, but it also has some interesting narrative history.

Other published histories cover some of our conference institutions, including Dr. Michael Wolfe's history, *In the World, Not of the World: 175 Years of the South Carolina United Methodist Advocate*, published in 2012, and *Daring Hearts and Spirits Free*, a history of South Carolina's United Methodist Women. And of course, many of our local churches have fine histories. One of the more recent overall histories of the conference was prepared by our current conference historian, Dr. A. V. Huff Jr. It is a much more modern history, and it was published as part of the 1985 edition of *United Methodist Ministers in South Carolina*. It is a much more readable narrative, and unlike some of the earlier works, it focuses on events that affected all Methodists rather than the leaders alone. For researchers looking for a good overview of the state's Methodist heritage, this would be a good place to start.

Before the 250th anniversary of Methodism in South Carolina in 2035, I hope someone will write a new, more comprehensive and complete story of Methodism in our state.

# Chapter 55

## Clergy Pictorial Directories

Since 1901, the South Carolina Conference has published clergy biographical directories about every ten years.

The first volume was called *Twentieth Century Sketches of the South Carolina Conference, M. E. Church, South* and was edited by Rev. Watson B. Duncan. The biographical sketches of each clergy member of the conference were often prepared by their friends and could be quite lengthy. These can be very useful for modern researchers, as they frequently mention the minister's accomplishments in the appointments where they served. Most, but not all, were accompanied by photographs. The volume began with an introduction by Wofford's then-president, Dr. James H. Carlisle, in which he referred to the book as a "family album." That seems an accurate description for a conference of not much larger than 200 members.

Duncan published a revised and expanded version of the volume in 1914. He was collecting information for a new edition when he died, at which point his family gave the information he had collected to the editor of the *Advocate*. The 1930 Annual Conference asked a group of ministers to work toward a new edition, and ultimately, the *Advocate* took on the project. The directory evolved into something more: a short history of the South Carolina and Upper South Carolina conferences and their institutions. Published in 1932 as *Builders: Sketches of Methodist Preachers in South Carolina with Historical Data*, the volume contained photographs, shorter biographical sketches, and an additional fifty pages of history and data.

From that point forward, a directory emerged about every ten years through the 1960s, with biographies in the front and separate glossy photographs in the back. The merger of the 1866 and 1785 conferences delayed production of the 1970s volume until 1975, and the format returned to that of the early 1930s, with sketches and photographs side by side. The 1985 edition, celebrating the bicentennial of American Methodism, contained a ninety-page history of Methodism in South Carolina, prepared by Dr. A. V. Huff Jr. Subsequent editions of the directory emerged in 1991 and 2001, though all the post-1961 directories had increasingly smaller photographs and shorter biographies.

The day of printed directories, however, appears to be in the past. Today, to find photographs or other information, one would need to look at the conference website.

Over the past few years, the conference archives at Wofford has made these directories available online. First, we focused on the photos, making the images from the 1901 through 1961 directories available on the web. We also had a late nineteenth-century photo album that we scanned and made available. That's the William Wynn Mood photo album, and it has photos of some late nineteenth-century clergy that are otherwise unavailable. Student workers along with Rev. Luther Rickenbaker, senior research associate in the archives, helped prepare short biographies to accompany the online photos. These photographs have helped local churches as they've worked on publishing histories or displaying photos of former ministers. All of these can be found on the Methodist archives website.

However, we always wanted to make the full directories available so that researchers, local church historians, and others could examine the full biographies of our clergy. We've posted the 1901, 1914, 1932, 1942, 1952, 1961, and 1975 directories on Wofford's digital repository site, which is located at https://digitalcommons.wofford.edu/methodistdirectories. The files are fairly large, so it might take a few moments to download them.

## Chapter 56

### Conference Journals

If getting your conference journal in the mail excites you, then this announcement should make your heart strangely warmed. The back issues of the *Annual Conference Journal*, all the way back to the early 1800s, are available online.

In the summer of 2020, with archival support money from apportionment dollars, the conference archives at Wofford was able to have the entire run of South Carolina conference journals digitized. Since these documents came back from the vendor, I've been working to get them ready to go online. This involved running optical character recognition software on each issue so they can be searched, creating a record for each journal, uploading them to a website, and then importing them to the site where researchers can view them.

Years ago, all the journals from the former 1785 conference and the Upper South Carolina Conference, which existed from 1915 to 1947, were microfilmed. The 1866 Conference journals were also microfilmed by another institution, and so we were able to have each of those sets digitized from the microfilm. The issues of the journal since 2006 are what archivists call "born-digital," which means they had a digital version from the very beginning. The various journals all live on Wofford's online digital repository, which Wofford pays for each year. I've completed most of the work of cataloging and uploading, and am happy to announce that you can find them online at https://digitalcommons.wofford.edu/methodistjournals.

Because the three predecessor conferences were different organizations, I've arranged the journals into four different sets—one for the 1785 Conference, one for the 1866 Conference, one for the Upper South Carolina Conference, and one for the current conference, which dates to 1972.

The collection is not 100 percent complete. The 1866 conference set stops at 1962, so we need to find the years 1963 to 1971, digitize them, and get them posted to complete that series. The earliest editions, from about 1814 to 1830, are actually excerpts from the General Minutes of the Annual Conferences, which include minutes from each Annual Conference. We scanned and added the South Carolina section of the General Minutes from 1785 to 1814 to help complete the set.

So why is having access to older conference journals a good thing? It means that local church historians can look up statistical information about their church without having to come to the archives. It means if you have a clergy ancestor, you can find their obituary or memoir in the pages of the journal. If you're looking for the history of a conference agency, you can find its old reports. And if you're trying to trace someone's appointments, they are all there.

The journal is the record of each annual conference session's business. Obviously, we are bigger and more complex these days, and the conference journal runs much longer than it used to. The *1911 Journal* of the 1785 conference ran about 120 pages. The journal for 1842 runs about twenty-four pages.

Putting these journals online has been a long-term goal, and we're glad to make them more widely available, as they help us build our connection between the past, the present, and the future.

# Chapter 57

## Historic Places in South Carolina

What makes a place historic? Is it merely age? If something lasts a certain number of years, does that make it historic? Or does something become historic when significant events happen there?

The answer, truthfully, is that it's some of both, and maybe even more.

South Carolina is an old state, and we have dozens of historic Methodist churches and places. While every church building has special meaning to those who worship there, a percentage of these churches have, through longevity, earned some recognition as a historic site.

The Department of the Interior, working through the State Historic Preservation Office, recognizes sites that have historical and architectural significance through listing them on the National Register of Historic Places. The United Methodist Church, through its conference and general commission on Archives and History, can recognize sites for their contribution to Methodist history in our conference. Some sites may also qualify for a historic marker through the South Carolina Department of Archives and History's highway marker program. More than one hundred Methodist places in South Carolina have one of these three recognitions, and some have more than one of them.

Generally, sites are listed because of their association with an event, development or personality with significant historic significance to the history of the annual conference. A National Register site generally has a strong connection to the broad contours of American history, and with churches, generally they have some architectural significance. Sometimes a congregation itself might be one hundred or 150 years old, but it is in a building that is only fifty or sixty years old. That wouldn't really be a historic church building, though the congregation's impact on its community over its long history was no doubt profound.

Several years ago, James A. Neal sought to compile all the historic sites in South Carolina Methodism into one book. This book, *Historic United Methodist Churches and Places in South Carolina*, was published in 2010, with a subsequent second printing. The book contains at least one photograph of each of the 108 churches or places that are on one of those three lists. It also contains some of each church's history

This summer, Jim Neal allowed us to post the full text of his book to our digital repository, where anyone can download and enjoy it. Here is the link: https://digitalcommons.wofford.edu/methodistbooks/9. From this work, we built a collection with an entry for each church along with photographs. It is available here, and they are arranged alphabetically by church name: https://digitalcommons.wofford.edu/umcschistoric.

Along with his collaborator Bill Segars, Neal has recently produced a second book, *Churches in South Carolina Burned During the American Revolution, a Pictorial Guide*. Most of these churches are Anglican, Presbyterian, or Congregational, as the American Revolutionary War predates the organization of Methodism in South Carolina. If you're interested, you can find it on Amazon.

# About the Author

Born in Spartanburg, Dr. Phillip Stone grew up in Bethel United Methodist Church. He graduated from Wofford College with Phi Beta Kappa honors, magna cum laude, in 1994. While a student, he worked in the college and Methodist archives with Dr. Herbert Hucks, himself a member of Bethel and a 1934 Wofford graduate. There, Phillip began to immerse himself in college and Methodist history. He also studied South Carolina history with Dr. Lewis Jones, a member of Central Church and a legendary figure in South Carolina and Methodist history. Phillip went on to earn his MA in history at the University of Georgia in 1996 and his PhD in history at the University of South Carolina in 2003, but not before returning to succeed Dr. Hucks as college and conference archivist at Wofford in March 1999.

While at Wofford, Phillip has worked to make the archives available to a wider audience, putting significant parts of the collection online for researchers around the state, but also processing collections and answering hundreds of reference questions a year. In addition to his work in the archives, he has taught southern politics, South Carolina politics, and modern western civilization. He's taught in Wofford's Lifelong Learning program for older adults. In 2010, he published a pictorial history of Wofford College.

In the community, he has served as president of the Hampton Heights Neighborhood Association twice, as a member and chair of the City of Spartanburg's Board of Architectural Design and Historic Review, and as a member and chair of the City of Spartanburg Planning Commission. At Bethel United Methodist Church, he has been the church historian since 1999 and as a lay member of the South Carolina Annual Conference since 2002. He has served ex officio on the Commission on Archives and History, and from 2012-2021, served on the Board of Trustees of the *South Carolina United Methodist Advocate*.

www.ingramcontent.com/pod-product-compliance
Lightning Source LLC
Chambersburg PA
CBHW070544090426
42735CB00013B/3063